Dipladenia 'Amoena'

AN ILLUSTRATED GUIDE TO

FLOWERING

HOUSEPLANTS

How to enjoy year-round colour in your home
Featuring 150 plants

Aechmea chantinii

Catharanthus roseus

AN ILLUSTRATED GUIDE TO

FLOWERING

HOUSEPLANTS

How to enjoy year-round colour in your home
Featuring 150 plants

Jack Kramer

The Rutledge Press
New York, New York

A Salamander Book

Published by The Rutledge Press,
112 Madison Avenue,
New York, New York 10016

ISBN 0-8317-4854-0

© 1981 Salamander Books Ltd.,
27 Old Gloucester Street,
London WC1N 3AF, United Kingdom.

First printing 1981

Distributed by W.H. Smith
Publishers Inc.,
112 Madison Avenue,
New York, New York 10016

All correspondence concerning the
content of this volume should be
addressed to Salamander Books Ltd.

Publisher's note: The material in
this book has previously appeared in
Growing Beautiful Flowers Indoors

Contents

The plants are arranged in alphabetical order of Latin name.
Page numbers in **bold** refer to text entries; those in *italics* refer to photographs.

Credits

Author: Jack Kramer, known throughout the world for his easy, familiar writing style, is the author of over 50 popular books on gardening subjects. Mr. Kramer writes from the personal experience of many successful years growing both indoor and outdoor plants.

Consultant: Sue Minter, a qualified horticulturalist, has edited and contributed to several plant books.

Editor: Geoff Rogers

Line drawings: Tyler/Camoccio Design Consultants
© Salamander Books Ltd.
Photographs: A full list of credits is given on page 160.
Colour reproductions: Scansets Ltd., Middlesex, England. Bantam Litho Ltd., Essex, England.
Monochrome: Tenreck, London, England.
Filmset: SX Composing Ltd., Essex, England.

Printed in Belgium by
Henri Proost et Cie, Turnhout.

Guzmania lingulata 'Minor Orange'

Introduction

There is nothing quite so disappointing as watching a cherished houseplant slowly dying in your care. Despite all your efforts, it never seems to regain the vitality it once enjoyed in the plant shop. Not surprisingly, this experience may persuade you that you will never succeed with any plants in your home. This is regrettable, because with just a little encouragement and the suggestion of a plant more suited to your home conditions, you might well become a successful and even a fanatic houseplant grower.

Whether you are one of life's 'plant refugees' or able to grow a wide range of houseplants with consummate skill, this guide will give you the incentive to try something new. Here is a selection of over 150 flowering houseplants, described with enthusiasm as well as accuracy, that can fill your home with colour all year through. The plants are presented in alphabetical order of Latin name and coded in words (not confusing symbols) according to their ideal growing temperature (see below), their degree of difficulty (For beginners, For everyone, For a challenge), and their willingness to bloom (Easy to bloom, Difficult to bloom). Clear instructions on the best way to grow each plant are followed, where appropriate, by a special tip to encourage flowering.

Each plant is illustrated by a clear line drawing and 120 of the plants are shown in beautiful colour photographs. Text and photographs are cross-referenced throughout (24♦) and an index of common names completes the book.

Temperature code
- Cool conditions 55–65°F (13–18°C)
- Intermediate conditions 65–75°F (18–24°C)
- Warm conditions 75–80°F (24–27°C)

Above: **Abutilon 'Boule de Neige'**
*Well known for their paper-thin
orange, yellow or red flowers,
abutilons are decorative plants
where a vertical accent is necessary.
Do stake plants so they do not
become unwieldy.* 17♦

Left: **Acacia armata**
*Grown more outdoors than indoors,
this beautiful yellow flowering plant is
a happy choice if you have space for
it. Flowers appear in early spring and
assure color at the window.* 17♦

Right: **Acalypha hispida**
*The long chenillelike red catkins
make A. hispida a popular houseplant. The large leaves are
decorative as well, and when young
a fine plant for limited space.* 18♦

Left: **Achimenes hybrids 'Paul Arnold'**
Dozens of attractive varieties come from this large gesneriad group, and all offer a wealth of colorful flowers for summer show. 18⬦

Below left: **Aechmea chantinii**
Called the 'Queen of the Bromeliads', A. chantinii has handsome broad leaves, rosette growth and an inflorescence that seems artificial, it is so vividly colored. Bracts last for months. 19⬦

Right: **Adenium obesum 'Multiflorum'**
An extraordinary succulent with rosettes of leaves and large white, crimson-edged flowers. The stems eventually become woody trunks of a sculpturesque form. 19⬦

Below; **Aeschynanthus lobbianus**
Brilliant red flowers in tubular 'lipstick cases' adorn this plant in midsummer – a mature specimen may have over 50 flowers. The plant has pendent growth and is best grown in a basket container. 20⬦

11

Left: Anguloa clowesii
The yellow tulip orchid is aptly named. Its fragrant blooms cluster at the base of the plant, but are never hidden from view because the leaves are upright. 22▸

Right: Angraecum eburneum
Large white to pale green crystalline flowers in autumn make this orchid highly desirable for indoor accent, and the evergreen straplike leaves are attractive as well. Blooms readily indoors. Very handsome. 22▸

Below: Alpinia purpurata
A fine ginger plant – though somewhat large – with dense clusters of red bracts; an excellent touch of tropical atmosphere for a spacious window. 21▸

13

Above: **Aphelandra squarrosa 'Louisae'**
This fine houseplant from South America has stellar yellow flowers – a brilliant display at any window. A good plant for limited space. 24▸

Left: **Ardisia crispa/crenata**
An ardisia covered with red berries makes a fine winter gift. Leaves are dark green and handsome. This plant from the East Indies is always welcome in window gardens. 24▸

Right: **Anthurium andreanum**
An exotic anthurium from Central America, with its glossy green leaves this is a glamorous subject for a shady part of the indoor garden. It bears large flower spathes throughout the summer, and comes in white or shades of pink and red. 23▸

Above: **Begonia boweri**
*Long a favorite, the eyelash begonia has spectacular foliage and white or pale pink flowers that are a delight throughout summer and autumn.*26▶

Left: **Azalea indica**
Here is a plant that can brighten any autumn day. A compact shrub, it can be in flower for many weeks. 25▶

Abutilon hybrids
(Dollflower; flowering maple)
- ● **Intermediate temperaturo**
- ● **For everyone**
- ● **Easy to bloom**

This is an amenable houseplant that has treelike growth to about 48in (120cm). Related to hollyhocks, abutilons have maplelike leaves and bear paper-thin, 2in (5cm) bell shaped flowers in early spring; they last for 2 days. There are many hybrids with flowers in delicate shades of yellow, orange and red.

Grow these plants in equal parts of potting soil and sand at a bright and sunny exposure; water heavily in warm weather and feed every third watering with plant food. Do not feed in the winter. Repot yearly in early spring and be sure abutilons have at least two to three hours of sun daily. Plants have a tendency to legginess so must be cut back at least once a year to encourage bushiness. These plants require no special care.

To encourage bloom;
Keep plants in small pots – a 5–6in (12.5–15cm) clay pot is fine. 8♦

Acacia armata
(Kangaroo thorn; wattle)
- ● **Cool conditions**
- ● **For everyono**
- ● **Difficult to bloom**

A thorny shrub, the kangaroo thorn has flattened leaf stalks or simple leaves; in spring globular heads of rich yellow flowers are produced. It makes a small and attractive treelike plant indoors, reaching a height of about 48in (120cm).

Grow the kangaroo thorn in full sunlight in a rich mix of equal parts of potting soil and humus. Keep soil evenly moist all year but take care not to overwater; provide good ventilation to keep growing conditions cool. After flowering allow the plant to rest at 50°F (10°C). Prune back to 6–10in (15–25cm). Fertilize mildly 3 times a year during warm months, not at all the rest of the year. Rarely bothered by insects. Propagate by seeds in spring or from stem cuttings in the summer.

To encourage bloom:
Keep in full sun with good air movement. 8♦

Acalypha hispida
(Chenille plant; foxtails; red hot cat's tail)
- **Intermediate conditions**
- **For beginners**
- **Easy to bloom**

This is a showy plant with attractive, hairy green leaves and strings of red flowers that resemble a chenille texture. The flowers spring from leaf axils and may grow to 20in (50cm) in length. The chenille plant grows to a height of about 30in (75cm); flowers appear at intervals during summer.

Grow the chenille plant at a sunny window in a rich mix: use equal parts of soil and humus. Water heavily during warm weeks and keep humidity at about 40 percent for best growth. Fertilize every second watering during spring and summer but not at all the rest of the year. Start new plants from cuttings in autumn. For a handsome pleasing display grow several plants together in a 6in (15cm) container.

To encourage bloom:
Give plenty of water and sun. 9♦

Achimenes hybrids
(Cupid's bower; hot water plant)
- **Warm growing conditions**
- **For a challenge**
- **Difficult to bloom**

Offering a superb summer display of color, these members of the gesneriad family have been highly hybridized and there are dozens of varieties in a rainbow of colors available for summer blooming. Not to be missed.

Plants need full sun for bloom and a rich soil and humus mix. Start from tubers in early spring in 6–8in (15–20cm) pots; when 4–5in (10–12.5cm) high repot in separate containers. Some of the hybrids are compact, others make excellent basket plants, growing to 20in (50cm). Keep soil evenly moist at all times, using lime-free water, and when bloom is over, store pots indoors in a dim cool place. Repot in early spring in fresh soil. Keep plants misted to avoid red spider.

To encourage bloom:
Must have at least 4 hours of sun daily; keep humid. 10♦

Adenium obesum 'Multiflorum'
(Desert rose; impala lily)
- **Warm conditions**
- **For a challenge**
- **Difficult to bloom**

An East African plant, the impala lily is an attractive shrubby plant up to 24in (60cm) tall, with dark green fleshy leaves arranged spirally. Its lovely 1in (2.5cm) funnel shaped white flowers edged with crimson blaze with color in spring.

Grow this succulent plant in a sunny window. Use equal parts of sand and humus for potting. Water judiciously, never allowing the soil to become waterlogged; this plant prefers dryness. In early spring feed about 3 times at 2-week intervals. Do not feed during the rest of the year. In winter the plant loses its leaves; keep soil barely moist then. Adeniums appreciate heat – up to 78°F (26°C) during the day, 10°F (5°C) less at night. Plant can be obtained from specialty suppliers.

To encourage bloom:
Observe winter rest. 11♦

Aechmea chantinii
(Amazonian zebra plant; queen of the bromeliads)
- **Intermediate conditions**
- **For everyone**
- **Easy to bloom**

One of the most glamorous bromeliads, *A. chantinii* grows to about 40in (1m) with green and white banded leaves and a branched spike of fiery red bracts crowned in yellow – a stunning inflorescence, especially as bloom occurs in winter. Color remains until early spring.

Grow in bright indirect light in 4–5in (10–12.5cm) pots of medium-grade fir bark. Water moderately all year and keep 'vase' of plant filled with water; do not feed. Mist leaves with water occasionally. Plants are relatively free of insects and grow with little care.

Start new plants from offshoots; when they are 3–4in (7.5–10cm) high and fully rooted, cut them off and pot individually in fir bark.

To encourage bloom:
Use the 'apple-in-the-bag' method. Place the plant in a plastic bag with some ripening apples; the gases given off by the apples will encourage the plant to bloom. Alternatively, place a ripening apple in the central funnel of the plant. 10♦

19

Aechmea fasciata
(Exotic brush; silver vase; urn plant; vase plant)
● **Intermediate conditions**
● **For everyone**
● **Easy to bloom**

The most popular plant of the bromeliad group, this plant grows to 30in (75cm) with wide leathery leaves of green and frosty white. Tufted blue and pink flower heads appear in spring and last until summer, or even longer. Plants are compact, vase shaped, beautiful.

Grow the urn plant in bright indirect light in 3–4in (7.5–10cm) clay pots filled with medium-size fir bark. Water moderately all year but keep 'vase' of plant filled with water at all times, except when the temperature falls below 55°F (13°C). Do not feed. Mist foliage occasionally; plants are almost pest-free – the leaves are too tough.

Start new plants from rooted offshoots; when they are 3–4in (7.5–10cm) high cut them off and pot in individual containers of bark.

To encourage bloom:
Use the 'apple-in-the-bag' method.

Aeschynanthus lobbianus
(Basket vine; lipstick vine)
● **Warm conditions**
● **For a challenge**
● **Difficult to bloom**

This summer-flowering gesneriad is a trailing plant up to 36in (90cm) long, with dark green leaves and clusters of brilliant red flowers at the tips of the stems – very colorful for basket growing.

Plants need bright light but no sun, which can scorch the leaves and dry out the plant. Grow in a porous mixture of equal parts of soil and humus. In active growth give plants plenty of water and mist them to keep humidity high (about 50 percent). Feed only once a month with plant food. Occasionally attacked by mealy bug; use old-fashioned methods to eradicate. New plants from cuttings taken in early spring.

To encourage bloom:
Keep humidity high. Rest the plant at 55°F (13°C) during the winter, keeping it rather dry. 11♦

Allamanda cathartica
(Common allamanda; golden trumpet)
- **Warm conditions**
- **For a challenge**
- **Difficult to bloom**

If you have room, this tropical evergreen climber up to 15ft (4.6m) has tubular waxy golden-yellow giant flowers in late spring and early summer that dazzle the eye. Puts on a spectacular display at any window.

The golden trumpet needs sun, so a sunny window is necessary; pot in large tubs of rich soil; a standard houseplant soil is fine, with added humus. Flood plants and then allow to dry out before watering again. Feed every second watering (these are greedy plants) except in autumn and winter. Rest after flowering and in winter cut back by one third and repot. Take stem cuttings in early spring for new plants.

To encourage bloom:
Repot annually to next pot size.

Alpinia purpurata
(Red ginger)
- **Warm conditions**
- **For a challenge**
- **Difficult to bloom**

From the ginger family, this showy 5ft (1.5m) plant with large leaves and boat shaped red bracts makes a brilliant summer display at the window. The tiny white flowers are hidden in the bracts. A fine addition to the indoor garden if you have space, and of good color.

Grow ginger at your sunniest window; plants need 3 hours of sun a day to bear flowers. Pot in a loose mix of equal parts of soil and humus that drains readily. Flood plants with water during warm weather; allow to rest slightly at other times, with less moisture. Use large tubs. Feed twice weekly; these are greedy plants. They need a good amount of heat during the day to prosper. New plants from division of rhizomes.

To encourage bloom:
Give plenty of water and sun. 13♦

Angraecum eburneum
(Comet orchid)
- **Intermediate conditions**
- **For everyone**
- **Easy to bloom**

A large orchid up to 36in (90cm), this fine plant has long leathery dark green leaves and large crystalline white to pale green flowers with spurs on tall scapes. Plants may have as many as 20 flowers in the autumn, an excellent addition to the indoor garden.

Grow the comet orchid in a bright but not sunny window; sun may harm this plant. Use large-grade fir bark for potting mix, and clay pots (plastic ones hold moisture too long for these orchids, which are sensitive to overwatering). Do not feed, but repot every second year in fresh bark. Provide good humidity – at least 30 percent.

When flower scapes appear in autumn be careful not to wet them, because rot can occur; and keep plants out of drafts. Leaves occasionally form patches of black but this will not harm the plant; trim away dead tissue. New plants can be obtained from offshoots.

To encourage bloom:
No special requirements. 13♦

Anguloa clowesii
(Yellow tulip orchid)
- **Intermediate conditions**
- **For everyone**
- **Easy to bloom**

This spectacular 20in (50cm) orchid has papery green leaves, and tulip shaped vivid chrome yellow flowers in summer – as many as 5 or 6 fragrant blooms per plant. This very handsome orchid is easy to bring into bloom indoors.

Grow the yellow tulip orchid at a bright window – bright light is needed but no sun. Use clay pots and medium-grade fir bark. Water evenly throughout the year; too much water can harm the plant. Do not feed. Provide ample ventilation and humidity. Temperature fluctuations can harm the plant. New plants from suppliers.

To encourage bloom:
Do not overwater. 12♦

Anthurium andreanum

(Flame plant; flamingo flower; pigtail plant; tail flower; painter's palette)
- ● **Warm conditions**
- ● **For beginners**
- ● **Easy to bloom**

This very popular plant grows up to about 24in (60cm) and has rich green elongated heart-shaped leaves and waxy white or coral colored flower spathes.

Anthuriums need a shady place to thrive. Use a potting mix of equal parts of soil and humus that drains readily. Apply water so that the soil is evenly moist all year, but take care as overwatering can harm plants. Adequate humidity (60 percent) is necessary for good growth, so mist plants frequently during warm weather. Feed about once a month during the growing season, not at all in winter. Provide warmth – at least 75°F (24°C) by day. Propagate from seeds or by dividing plants.

To encourage bloom:
Keep humidity high. 15♦

Anthurium scherzerianum

(Flame plant; flamingo flower; pigtail plant; tail flower)
- ● **Warm conditions**
- ● **For beginners**
- ● **Easy to bloom**

From Central and South America, these 20in (50cm) plants have a flower spathe of brilliant red, which appears lacquered and lasts for weeks. Flower spathes may appear throughout the year. A striking display.

Grow the flamingo flower in a shady place for best results. Use a porous mixture of equal parts of soil and humus, and keep the soil quite moist in the warm months and, somewhat drier in winter months, but never bone dry. Plants need higher than average temperatures – at least 78–82°F (26–28°C) to thrive – and sufficient humidity (50 percent). Mist with water frequently. Start new plants from offsets or seed.

To encourage bloom:
Keep humidity high.

Aphelandra squarrosa 'Louisae'
(Saffron spike; zebra plant)
● **Warm conditions**
● **For a challenge**
● **Difficult to bloom**

This is certainly a beautiful aphelandra, with shiny corrugated leaves, and yellow bracts in summer. The plant grows to about 20in (50cm) – a good small subject for the window garden.

Aphelandras need a sunny place. Grow in small pots of rich soil; use equal parts of humus and packaged soil. Keep evenly moist all year; feed every 2 weeks in warm weather. Plants grow rapidly and are quite thirsty; they wilt severely if not given enough water so care is necessary to grow them properly. In winter they tend to get leggy, so start new ones from cuttings each spring.

To encourage bloom:
Rest for 4 to 6 weeks in a cooler temperature after flowering. 14♦

Ardisia crispa/crenata
(Coral berry; spear flower)
● **Intermediate conditions**
● **For everyone**
● **Easy to bloom**

This showy 20in (50cm) plant has small berries following tiny sweet-scented white or rose flowers in summer. Leaves are scalloped and dark green. It is very ornamental in its season and easy to grow indoors.

In summer protect *Ardisia* from strong sun but in winter the plant can be grown at a sunny window. Use a rich potting soil of equal parts of soil and humus. Drainage must be almost perfect. Give plenty of moisture all year except in winter. Feed monthly during the warm months. Do not feed when flowers appear; this will discourage the formation of berries. After a few years, start new plants from cuttings; the old ones get straggly.

To encourage bloom:
Give plenty of water. 14♦

Astrophytum asterias
(Sand dollar cactus; sea urchin cactus; star cactus)
- ● **Intermediate conditions**
- ● **For beginners**
- ● **Difficult to bloom**

Easy to grow, this almost spineless star shaped cactus has 2in (5cm) yellow flowers with red centers in spring or summer. Growing only 3in (7.5cm) across and 1in (2.5cm) tall, it is a fine plant if space on your windowsill is limited.

The star cactus needs sun, so place it at a sunny window. Grow in equal parts of sand and soil, and be sure drainage is perfect. Keep evenly moist all year except in winter, when plants can be grown somewhat dry but not bone dry. Do not feed or mist. *A. asterias* is one of the most attractive astrophytums. Propagate by seed in the spring.

To encourage bloom:
Give plenty of sun and a cool resting period in winter.

Azalea indica
(Rhododendron simsii)
(Indian azalea)
- ● **Cool conditions**
- ● **For a challenge**
- ● **Difficult to bloom**

A fine small-leaved evergreen shrub, *Azalea indica* makes a handsome tub plant, with brilliant white, pink, red or purple flowers from midsummer to winter. The plant will eventually grow to about 30in (75cm) – a handsome accent for cool indoor gardens.

Grow this plant at a bright window – sun is not necessary. Use a rich potting soil of equal parts of humus and standard houseplant mix. Water heavily most of the year with lime-free water, but after bloom taper off moisture and keep the soil just barely moist. Cut back to 4–6in (10–15cm) and resume watering when growth starts. Feed every 2 weeks during growth; not at all the rest of the year.

Azaleas require the coolest place at your window and need frequent misting to keep humidity high (about 40 percent). New plants should be bought from suppliers.

To encourage bloom:
Observe resting time. Never allow soil to dry out. Put plant outside in a cool, moist place through the warm summer months. 16♦

Begonia boweri
(Eyelash begonia; miniature eyelash begonia)
● **Warm conditions**
● **For everyone**
● **Easy to bloom**

This charming miniature, up to 14in (35cm) tall, bears lovely white or pink flowers, but is best known for its exquisite foliage – delicate green leaves edged with black markings like an eyelash. Of the rhizomatous group, *B. boweri* is sure to please any gardener.

Grow the eyelash begonia at a west or east window – bright light is fine; sun is not needed except in winter. The potting mix should be porous and rich – use standard houseplant soil and add half a cup of humus for a 5in (12.5cm) pot. Let soil dry out thoroughly between waterings and give less moisture in winter. Feed in active growth. Rhizomatous begonias are food storehouses, so this plant can tolerate some drought if necessary. propagate by division or cuttings.

To encourage bloom:
Allow to grow potbound. 16◗

Begonia 'Fireglow'
● **Intermediate conditions**
● **For a challenge**
● **Difficult to bloom**

One of the newer begonias, this plant blooms over a long period of time in summer and autumn with handsome red flowers. Leaves are bright green and plants grow to about 16in (40cm). For all its beauty however, this can be a temperamental plant. Needs care.

Grow this begonia at a bright location where there is neither too much sun nor too much shade. Use a potting soil of equal parts humus and soil that drains readily. Feed every 2 weeks in the growing season – not at all rest of year. To keep plant in fine stead, dry off slightly after bloom time for about 3 to 5 weeks with just scant moisture; then resume watering. Do not mist or get water on the leaves. New plants from cuttings.

To encourage bloom:
Observe resting time after flowering period, with little moisture.

Begonia 'Orange Rubra'

(Angelwing begonia)
- Intermediate conditions
- For everyone
- Easy to bloom

This angelwing begonia with pretty orange flowers and wing shaped leaves bears flowers in spring. The fibrous rooted plant grows to 36in (90cm) and can reach to 6ft (1.8m) if conditions are ideal. Very pretty.

For angelwings, a sunny location is needed. Grow in equal parts of soil and humus kept well watered during the warm months – less water in winter is fine. Feed every month. Prune occasionally to keep plants within bounds – cut back to about one third original size in late autumn. Cuttings can be taken in early spring for new plants.

To encourage bloom:
Give at least 4 hours of sun a day, and keep well ventilated. 33♦

Begonia semperflorens

(Wax begonia)
- Intermediate conditions
- For beginners
- Easy to bloom

These small plants make a handsome accent in the window garden. Growing to 14in (35cm) tall, wax begonias are available in several colors, white and red being the most popular. Leaves are dark green or mahogany colored. Nice small plants for colorful summer flowers.

Grow wax begonias in filtered sun. Use a potting mix of equal parts of humus and houseplant soil that drains well. Small pots are best for these plants. Although the plants require copious watering in their growing season (warm months) they must never become waterlogged. Feed every 2 weeks while plants are in active growth; in late autumn and winter allow the plants a rest, and to dry out somewhat.

Provide good air circulation and keep a lookout for thrips, which sometimes attack begonias – use appropriate remedies when necessary. Prune back tops when plants get leggy. Propagate by cuttings or seed.

To encourage bloom:
Give plenty of light. 33♦

Beloperone guttata (Drejella)
(Shrimp plant)
● **Intermediate conditions**
● **For beginners**
● **Easy to bloom**

Paper-thin, flesh-colored bracts that overlap like a shrimp's body give this plant its common name; the leaves are dark green. The shrimp plant grows to about 36in (90cm) and makes a handsome display in early spring. The white flowers, almost hidden by the bracts, do not last long but bloom occurs over a long period of time, well into autumn.

You can grow the shrimp plant at almost any window and it will still bloom. It is not fussy about soil, but needs even moisture all year. Plants do not need feeding – they grow by themselves, practically. Prune back leggy growth in early summer – remove the top 8–10in (20–25cm) of the plant to encourage bushiness. Propagate by stem cuttings. A yellow variety has recently been introduced, and is quite stunning.

To encourage bloom:
Good light and some sun produces richer colored bracts.

Billbergia pyramidalis
(Queen's tears; summer torch)
● **Intermediate conditions**
● **For everyone**
● **Easy to bloom**

A 30in (90cm) popular bromeliad with golden-green leaves, and orange-pink bracts and red and blue flowers in midsummer – a treat at any window. Flowers are short lived but a mature plant bears several spikes.

Grow *B. pyramidalis* at a west or east window. Use a potting mix of equal parts of lime-free soil and medium-grade fir bark, packed tightly. Clay pots are best -- plants become top heavy in plastic ones. Keep 'vase' of plant filled with water, and the bark moderately moist all year. Use lime-free water. Feeding is unnecessary. This plant is rarely bothered by insects and requires repotting every second year. New plants from offshoots in spring.

To encourage bloom:
Use the 'apple-in-the-bag' method. Place the plant in a plastic bag with some ripening apples; the gases given off by the apples will encourage the plant to bloom. Alternatively, place a ripening apple in the central funnel of the plant for the same effect. 34●

Bougainvillea
(Paper flower)
● **Warm conditions**
● **For a challenge**
● **Difficult to bloom**

Bougainvillea indoors? Why not. This climbing plant bears handsome red or purple bracts in midsummer (the flowers are insignificant) and needs space, for it grows to 6ft (1.8m) or more if conditions suit it. It responds well to pruning to size, however; this should be done immediately after flowering. The leaves are handsome, mid or dark green in colour. A great basket plant.

Grow bougainvillea at the sunniest window you have and use a rich potting soil. Add one cup of humus to an 8in (20cm) pot. Plants are greedy and need plenty of water and feeding every 2 weeks while in active growth, but no feeding in cool weather when the plant slows down; water sparingly then. The plants should be rested throughout the winter.

Be alert for red spider, which occasionally attacks plants – use a suitable chemical preventative or mist thoroughly to discourage infestation. Grow new plants from stem cuttings.

To encourage bloom:
Give at least 4 hours sun daily. 35◆

Bouvardia× domestica
(Jasmine plant; trompetilla)
● **Cool conditions**
◐ **For everyone**
● **Easy to bloom**

A shrub to 40in (1m), *B.×domestica* has oval leaves in twos or threes and clusters of brightly colored tubular fragrant flowers from summer to late autumn, making it a valuable asset in the window garden. Flower color is generally white, pink or red; there are many varieties.

Bouvardia needs a sunny window to bloom; pot in packaged soil that drains readily. Water freely in the warm months, but not so much the rest of the year. Feed monthly. Provide adequate humidity by misting the plant with tepid water. Easily grown. Propagate by stem cuttings in spring.

To encourage bloom:
Prune in late spring or early summer. Raise new plants every 2 years.

Brassavola nodosa
(Lady of the night)
- **Intermediate conditions**
- **For beginners**
- **Easy to bloom**

Browallia speciosa
- **Intermediate conditions**
- **For a challenge**
- **Difficult to bloom**

Producing an exquisite 3in (7.5cm) dazzling white heavily scented flower, *B. nodosa* grows only 10–14in (25–35cm) tall, and has terete type (pencil-like) leaves. The plant puts on its show in autumn, one flower following another for several weeks. The flowers are particularly fragrant at night.

Grow the lady of the night at an east or west window; use medium-grade fir bark and 4–5in (10–12.5cm) pots. Keep the plant moderately moist at all times and be careful to ensure that air circulation is good. Mist occasionally. Do not feed. Be sure drainage is good and do not pamper this plant – it grows almost by itself. Propagate by division.

To encourage bloom:
Dry out slightly for about 3 weeks in autumn to encourage buds. 34◆

Glossy leaves, and violet funnel shaped flowers in summer, make this plant a joy to have indoors. Pinching the growing tips out will keep the plant to about 14in (35cm); otherwise it will grow to 24in (60cm). It takes some coaxing, but is not impossible to bloom. Worth a try. Best grown several to a tub for a handsome display. Many brightly colored hybrids are available.

Grow *Browallia* in a shady place; sun harms these plants. Use a potting mix of equal parts of humus and houseplant soil. Be sure drainage is good. Keep soil evenly moist – plants should never dry out. Feed every 2 weeks in summer months. Provide good air circulation and never allow temperatures to fall below 50°F (10°C). Propagate by seed in spring. Discard plants once flowering has finished.

To encourage bloom:
Keep soil evenly moist. Stick to the summer feeding program. 36◆

Calanthe vestita
● **Intermediate conditions**
● **For everyone**
● **Easy to bloom**

This 10in (25cm) orchid grows from a bulb and, if planted in spring, bears scalloped red and white flowers in midwinter – quite a treat. Once established the plant is really undemanding and grows easily.

Plant bulbs in equal parts of soil and fir bark in spring in 4in (10cm) clay pots; place at a west window until growth starts. Water judiciously at first. Increase watering as growth matures, then move to a bright and sunny window. Do not feed; do not spray with water. When leaves mature in autumn allow the plant to dry out somewhat but do not keep bone dry; reduce the temperature by 10°F (5°C) if possible. When buds form resume watering. After the flowers fade, let it dry out naturally and store pot and bulb in a dry shady place. Start plant again in fresh growing medium in spring.

To encourage bloom:
Follow rest periods. 36◗

Calceolaria hybrids
(Lady's pocketbook; lady's slippers; pocketbook plant; pouch flower; slipper flower; slipperwort)
● **Cool conditions**
● **For everyone**
● **Easy to bloom**

Though short lived – only a few months – these colorful 10in (25cm) annuals are popular and add a note of festivity to the window garden. Many hybrids are available in a variety of stunning colors from dark yellow to brilliant reds.

Grow at a sunny but cool window in a rich soil; keep moderately moist at all times. Do not feed. Sow seeds in spring or summer for new plants. Try to maintain cool temperatures: 55°F (13°C) for best growing. Will not succeed in heat. When flowering is over, discard plants.

To encourage bloom:
No special requirements.

Callistemon citrinus
(Bottlebrush; crimson bottlebrush)
● **Cool conditions**
● **For everyone**
● **Easy to bloom**

This slender shrub reaches 60in (1.5m), and has slender leaves and stunning red or yellow spikes of flowers with no petals, but long stamens. The brilliant red flowers appear in summer and autumn. Makes a handsome indoor subject grown in large tubs, if you have space for it.

Grow *Callistemon* in full sun for healthy plants. Use a standard packaged houseplant soil that drains readily. Allow to dry out between waterings and feed every 2 weeks in warm weather. Keep slightly dry in winter, but never bone dry. Spray occasionally with tepid water to maintain good humidity. This plant can tolerate heat or cold, but prefers a rest in winter at 50°F (10°C). New plants from stem cuttings in spring.

To encourage bloom:
Ensure good ventilation during the summer months. 37♦

Camellia japonica
(Common camellia; tea plant)
● **Cool conditions**
● **For a challenge**
● **Difficult to bloom**

For cool locations, camellias are worth their weight in gold because they bear handsome flowers – pink, white or red – and the season of bloom lasts from midwinter to spring. Plants will grow to 10ft (3m) or more.

Grow camellias in a bright window – east or west exposure – and use equal parts of garden loam, peat moss and sand for the soil mix. Acidity to pH 5.5 is essential. Give plenty of water; the soil should never dry out. Mist foliage every day in summer, about every other day the rest of the year. Use tepid, lime-free water for watering and misting. Apply an acid fertilizer during active growth in spring and keep humidity at about 50 percent. Repot only when absolutely necessary.

Watch for occasional attacks of red spider – grow with good air circulation to avoid pests. Bud drop is a common complaint indoors: too much water in cool weather hinders bud opening and too little water causes buds to drop. Grow new plants from tip cuttings in spring.

To encourage bloom:
Ensure coolness: 50°F (10°C). 37♦

Begonia semperflorens
*Long an outdoor favorite, the wax
begonia is small and pretty. The
flowers appear on and off for many
months, making it a valuable asset in
the indoor garden.* 27♦

Below: **Begonia 'Orange Rubra'**
*A fine angelwing begonia with
handsome leaves spotted in white,
and cascades of orange flowers.* 27♦

Above: **Brassavola nodosa**
Small but with charm, this orchid has needlelike leaves and heavenly scented white flowers that perfume the whole room at night. 30♦

Left: **Billbergia pyramidalis**
Golden-green leaves and orange-pink flower bracts make this easy to grow bromeliad a favorite. 28♦

Right: **Bougainvillea**
This popular red or purple flowering climbing plant is perfect for the sunny window. With careful culture it will bloom freely throughout the summer. Needs support; very tropical and pretty. 29♦

Above: **Browallia speciosa**
*This delightful plant is now available
in compact hybrids that flower freely.
They can be placed outdoors during
the summer months.* 30♦

Below: **Calanthe vestita**
*Do not let the fact that this orchid is
deciduous deter you; it makes up for
its bareness in winter with dainty
pink-purple and white blooms.* 31♦

Above: **Callistemon citrinus**
*Brilliant color makes Callistemon a
popular plant, but it is large and
requires space. Blooming in summer
or autumn and rather unusual, it adds
interest to the indoor garden.* 32♦

Right: **Camellia japonica**
*Many varieties of fine flowering
evergreens for that cool location.
Flower colors range from white to
red. Outstanding.* 32♦

Above: **Cattleya
Bob Betts 'Mont Millais'**
*Known as the corsage flower,
cattleyas are always sure to please
the indoor gardener. The flowers are
large and generally fragrant. C. Bob
Betts 'Mont Millais' is a fine white and
a parent of many cattleyas.* 50♦

Left: **Capsicum annuum**
*This lovely decorative plant has
handsome brilliant red, yellow or
purple fruit in winter.* 49♦

Above: **Catharanthus roseus**
*Rose red flowers in summer make
this a fine seasonal plant for indoors.*

*New plants are best started from
cuttings or seed each year. Unusual
and worth the space.* 50♦

Above: **Celosia argentea
'Pyramidalis'**
*The red or yellow flowers resemble
plumes. An ideal plant for the
windowsill, as dwarf varieties grow to
only 12in (30cm). Generally pale
green, the leaves of some varieties
are a beautiful bronze.*51♦

Above: **Columnea microphylla**
*With tiny leaves and bright scarlet
and yellow flowers, this trailing
gesneriad creates a sensation.
Needs warm, humid conditions.* 56♦

Below: **Citrus mitis**
*A handsome small tree, C. mitis
bears tiny oranges in winter, making it
a decorative windowsill plant. Ideal
for small places. Easy to grow.* 53♦

Above: **Coelogyne ochracea**
Pretty as a picture, this dainty harbinger of spring has yellow and white flowers. A fine orchid. 55♦

Left: **Crocus**
Yellow crocuses are usually the earliest to bloom of the large-flowered varieties. Bring them into the warm only when the buds begin to show color. 57♦

Right: **Clivia miniata**
If you can't grow anything, this plant will make you a gardener. Easy to bloom each spring with magnificent clusters of orange flowers. Handsome straplike dark green leaves. Highly recommended. 54♦

Above: **Cymbidium hybrids**
This large group of orchids offers handsome long-lasting flowers in an array of colors. Plants come in standard sizes up to 48–60in (120–150cm) or in miniature (up to 24in, 60cm) for those with limited window space. The miniature hybrid shown here is called Elmwood, an easy to grow and very elegant variety. 59♦

Left: **Cuphea ignea**
The black and white ashlike tips of the red tubular flowers give this abundantly blooming plant its common name of cigar plant. 58♦

Right: **Cyclamen**
Cyclamen grow wild in Greece and along the eastern shores of the Mediterranean. Hybrids from these are highly prized indoor flowering plants. They come in beautiful pastel shades; always desirable. 58♦

Above: **Echinocereus baileyi**
A lovely 8in (20cm) cylindrical cactus with violet-pink flowers. 61♦

Below: **Echeveria 'Doris Taylor'**
Perhaps the best known of the echeverias, with handsome spoon shaped foliage and red and yellow flowers in spring. 60♦

Above right:
Dendrobium 'Gatton Sunray'
This colorful dendrobium is hard to resist. With a little extra care the plant will bloom twice a year. 59♦

Right: **Epidendrum cochleatum**
The clamshell orchid is easy to grow and a favorite for unusual flowers. 62♦

Above: **Episcia cupreata**
This is one of the popular episcias, with fine scarlet flowers and leaves that look sugar-coated. 63▶

Left: **Episcia dianthiflora**
From tropical Mexico, this white flowering episcia is a favorite houseplant; decorative foliage adds to its appeal. Use it in hanging containers for maximum display. 63▶

Campanula isophylla
(Bellflower; Italian bellflower;
star of Bethlehem;
trailing campanula)
● **Cool conditions**
● **For beginners**
● **Easy to bloom**

These plants are rewarding for
basket growing, with trailing stems
up to 20in (50cm) long, covered with
white or blue flowers from
midsummer until early winter. A
mature plant has hundreds of
flowers.

Campanulas need plenty of light
and require good circulation of air to
thrive. Shade from direct sun in
summer. Use standard potting mix;
be sure drainage is perfect. Water
heavily and then allow soil to dry out
between waterings. In winter, when
growth is slow, cut back to about 5in
(12.5cm); keep on dry side and cool
(55°F, 13°C). In spring, repot in
fresh soil and increase moisture.
New plants from cuttings.

To encourage bloom:
Pick off flowers as they fade; seed
formation reduces bloom. Old plants
decline in flowering vigor; replace
with young cuttings.

Capsicum annuum
(Ornamental chilli; red pepper plant)
● **Cool conditions**
● **For beginners**
● **Easy to bloom**

This is a delightful winter plant
with small summer flowers followed
by red autumn fruits shaped like
miniature peppers that last through
the cold months. Plants grow to 9–
14in (23–35cm) tall – fine small
companions for larger houseplants
at windows. Many hybrids are
available with different colored fruits.

Give the red pepper plant a
window where there is full sun – it
needs all the light it can get. Grow in
standard packaged houseplant soil
kept evenly moist all year. Grow cool
(60°F, 16°C) or the ornamental fruit
drops. Do not feed. This plant lasts
only one year, but it is worth its space
at the window because of its good
color and handsome foliage. Start
new plants from seed in spring;
warmth is needed to germinate them.

To encourage bloom and fruit:
Give ample sun and ventilation.
Spray flowers with water once a day
to help the fruit to set. 38♦

Catharanthus roseus
(Vinca rosea)
(Madagascar periwinkle)
- **Intermediate conditions**
- **For beginners**
- **Easy to bloom**

This 14in (35cm) plant has dark green glossy leaves, and rose-red or red-centered white flowers in summer, making it a handsome addition to the indoor garden. Excellent seasonal color.

Grow the Madagascar periwinkle in full sun. Use standard houseplant soil kept evenly moist all year. Be sure drainage is good. Feed every 2 weeks during warm months. Use small pots for best results – grow several to a tub for a handsome display. Never allow temperature to go below 55°F (13°C). Start new plants every year from tip cuttings taken in spring or raise from seed.

To encourage bloom:
Ensure good ventilation. 39♦

Cattleya hybrids
(Corsage flower)
- **Intermediate conditions**
- **For everyone**
- **Easy to bloom**

These are a large and popular group of orchids, with leathery strap shaped leaves and exquisite flowers well known to the florist. Plants do bloom indoors and there are thousands of hybrids to choose from, in colors from white to pink and red. Great for that special place at the window. Flowering time depends on the variety. Superlative in the home.

Cattleyas need sun – indeed they must have a really bright, sunny exposure to bloom. Use a medium-grade fir bark or osmunda fiber for potting. Keep plants evenly moist all year – there is no specific drying out time necessary. Do not feed, as this can prevent blooming. Provide ample humidity (40 percent) and be sure there is a good circulation of air in the growing area. These are epiphytic plants and need a buoyant atmosphere to prosper. Plants are rarely bothered by insects. Blooming times depend on specific hybrids, with plants for all seasons. New plants from suppliers or division.

To encourage bloom:
Provide ample sun. 38♦

Celosia argentea
- **Intermediate conditions**
- **For beginners**
- **Easy to bloom**

This plant is available in two forms: 'Cristata' (cockscomb) with comblike crested flower heads in various colors, and 'Pyramidalis' (plume celosia, Prince of Wales' feathers) with plumed flowers in brilliant red or yellow. Both types have pale green leaves. 'Cristata' and the dwarf varieties of 'Pyramidalis' reach 12in (30cm) in height; other varieties of 'Pyramidalis' are larger and may reach 36in (90cm).

Grow *Celosia* in your sunniest window; use a standard packaged houseplant soil that drains well. Water freely most of the year except in winter, when moisture can be somewhat less. Feed monthly in warm weather. In winter allow to die back, and repot in fresh soil in spring. Otherwise, discard old plants and start afresh from seed.

To encourage bloom:
Always provide good ventilation. 40♦

Chamaecereus silvestrii
(Gherkin cactus, peanut cactus)
- **Warm conditions**
- **For beginners**
- **Easy to bloom**

Growing to 10in (25cm), this cactus has narrow cylindrical green branches with white spines. The flowers are 2in (5cm) across, brilliant orange-red and stunning, but last only a few days. Easy to grow, this is a good pot plant for beginners.

Grow the peanut cactus in full sun – without adequate sun the bloom will be sparse. Use a potting mix of equal parts of soil and sand that drains readily. Water sparingly – allow soil to dry out between waterings; overwatering will kill the plant. Do not feed. Keep in a well-ventilated place. Remove small branches and use as cuttings in spring for new plants.

To encourage bloom:
Give plenty of sun. Keep the plant very cool in winter (40°F, 4°C).

Chrysanthemum
(Florist's mum)
- **Cool conditions**
- **For beginners**
- **Easy to bloom**

Potted chrysanthemums of yellow, bronze, white, or red make beautiful plants at windows. There are many hybrids of these plants that make fine temporary seasonal plants for the home. The most popular types are the dwarf 'all the year round' chrysanthemums that reach 6–10in (15–25cm) and can provide flowers at any season.

Grow chrysanthemums at a bright but not sunny window; keep them as cool as possible: 60°F (16°C) is ideal. Use a rich soil and keep quite moist throughout blooming. After flowers fade, cut back to 2–4in (5–10cm) and set plants in a frost-free garage or cold frame with soil kept barely moist until spring; then set them in the garden. They can be potted and used again indoors the following season, although dwarfed varieties will grow to their usual height of up to 30in (75cm). Stem cuttings can be taken but, again, new plants may be larger and the compactness of dwarf varieties lost.

To encourage bloom:
Keep plants well watered.

Cineraria cruenta
- **Cool conditions**
- **For a challenge**
- **Difficult to bloom**

Also called *Senecio cruentus,* these are difficult plants to resist – they have flowers in vibrant shades of red, blue and purple in very early spring and bloom for about 2 to 3 weeks indoors. After flowers fade, they must be discarded; still they are worth their price for providing a stunning seasonal display.

Keep plants at a bright but not sunny window and soil should be watered evenly at all times. To keep plants blooming, maintain cool temperatures of, say, 55–60°F (13 – 16°C). Sun and warmth will desiccate cinerarias. Be careful of the cineraria mite, which is prevalent on plants – use any of the suitable pesticides with caution.

To encourage bloom:
Grow in coolness (45–50°F, 7–10°C) until flower buds form.

Citrus mitis
(Calamondin orange)
- **Warm conditions**
- **For everyone**
- **Easy to bloom**

This popular 30in (75cm) pot plant from the Philippines has small orange fruits and dark green oval leaves. Flowers are white and fragrant. Both flowers and fruit appear throughout the year, with the best display in winter.

Grow the calamondin orange in a sunny location. Use a potting mix of equal parts of humus and houseplant soil. Allow soil to dry out between waterings and feed every 2 weeks in the summer months. In winter allow soil to dry out somewhat and keep cooler (55°F, 13°C). Provide a buoyant atmosphere and mist leaves with water frequently to deter spider mites, which adore this little orange tree. Cut back each year to about 10in (25cm) to encourage new growth and a bushy habit. Get new plants from pips or cuttings.

To encourage bloom and fruit:
Give ample sun or plunge outdoors in full sun during the summer months. Plants need pollinating by hand to set fruit if you are unable to put them outdoors.41♦

Clerodendrum thomsoniae
(Bleeding heart vine; glory bower)
- **Intermediate conditions**
- **For everyone**
- **Easy to bloom**

True to its name this is a glory of a plant with large leaves and small but striking flowers – they are white and deep crimson, and appear in early spring and may last until autumn. Overlooked by most growers, this climbing plant is a fine addition to the window garden. Unpruned it will grow to 10ft (3m) in height. Very decorative as pot or basket plants.

Grow the glory bower in a bright window – east or west exposure. Use a porous soil of equal parts of humus and soil. Keep the soil evenly moist except in winter, when plants lose some leaves naturally and need little water. Feed every 2 weeks when in active growth. Cuttings root easily and bloom the first year. An outstanding plant.

To encourage bloom:
Prune after blooming to encourage young growth on which the next year's flowers will be borne.

Clivia miniata
(Kaffir lily)
- **Intermediate conditions**
- **For everyone**
- **Easy to bloom**

A fine bulbous plant, *C. miniata* has dark green straplike leaves, and handsome clusters of orange flowers in early spring that last for several days. Mature plants are a splendid sight in bloom. Many new hybrids are available.

Grow *Clivia* in a shady place; sun will harm the plants. Use a growing medium of equal parts of sand and soil. Keep soil evenly moist all year except in winter, when soil can be somewhat dry. Feed every 2 weeks in very early spring – not at all during the rest of the year. Leave bulbs in pots for several years – plants react adversely to repotting. New plants by division of bulbs in late winter.

To encourage bloom:
Grow potbound in 6 or 7in (15 or 18 cm) containers. Keep dry during the winter months. 43▶

Coelogyne cristata
- **Cool conditions**
- **For everyone**
- **Easy to bloom**

From the mountains of the Himalayas comes this fascinating 20in (50cm) orchid with grasslike leaves and dazzling showy white 4in (10cm) fragrant flowers. In midwinter the display is a beautiful sight.

Grow *C. cristata* at an east or west window and use medium-grade fir bark. Keep the bark moderately moist all year except after flowering, when a short 3 to 5 week rest with little water is advisable. Mist to keep humidity high and grow as cool as possible: 60°F (16°C) at night is fine. Do not feed. Rarely bothered by insects. New plants from suppliers.

To encourage bloom:
Observe rest after blooming time. Grow the plant in a cool place.

Coelogyne ochracea
- **Warm conditions**
- **For everyone**
- **Easy to bloom**

A springtime beauty, this 20in (50cm) orchid bears delicate yellow and white flowers in clusters; they are scented and beautiful. This is an easy orchid to grow and highly recommended; it should be grown more widely.

The plant will do well at a west or east exposure; grow in medium-grade fir bark, kept evenly moist all year. Needs some warmth: 75°F (24°C). Do not feed but mist with tepid water occasionally to maintain good humidity. New plants can be obtained from orchid suppliers.

To encourage bloom:
See that the plant has some sunshine during winter months. 42♦

Columnea×banksii
- **Warm conditions**
- **For a challenge**
- **Difficult to bloom**

This beautiful trailing gesneriad to 36in (90cm) has small oval green leaves, and lovely two-lipped scarlet flowers with yellow markings in summer. Ideal for basket growing.

Grow this plant at a bright window – sun is not necessary. Use equal parts of soil and humus and be sure the medium drains readily. A stagnant soil can cause harm to the plant. Water judiciously all year, keeping the soil just moist to the touch but never too dry or too wet. Feed during growth at every other watering. Adequate humidity is necessary for best growth – maintain 40 percent. Mist the plant with tepid water in hot weather. Grow new plants from tip cuttings.

To encourage bloom:
No special requirements.

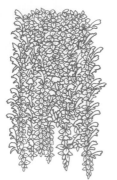

Columnea microphylla
(Goldfish vine; small-leaved goldfish vine)
● **Warm conditions**
● **For a challenge**
● **Difficult to bloom**

With tiny leaves and bright red and yellow flowers this trailing gesneriad can make any window a garden. The colorful display occurs in winter and spring and plants may have as many as 100 flowers. Grows to 48in (120cm).

A west or east exposure and a growing medium of equal parts of soil and humus are fine. Keep evenly moist all year and grow in warmth – 75°F (24°C). Coolness can inhibit growth. Feed every 2 weeks when in active growth and maintain a humidity of about 50 percent. Shade from summer sun. Propagate by taking tip cuttings in spring.

To encourage bloom:
Keep warm and humid; slightly drier in winter. Remove spent flowers to prevent berries forming, which waste the plant's energy. 41▶

Crassula falcata
● **Warm conditions**
● **For beginners**
● **Easy to bloom**

A large group of succulents originating from South Africa, most crassulas make excellent houseplants and this is no exception. With thick, gray, sickle shaped leaves and scarlet flowers, this plant grows to about 30in (75cm). Not spectacular, but handsome. A very amenable plant and sure to please.

You can grow this plant in full sun. Provide a well-drained potting soil: use equal parts of humus, soil, and perlite or gravel. Allow to dry out between waterings. Feed every 2 weeks in summer; not at all the rest of the year. Provide good air circulation – do not mist the leaves. Rarely bothered by insects. New plants can be started each year from stem or leaf cuttings or seed.

To encourage bloom:
Provide full sun and keep cooler (55°F, 13°C) in winter.

Crocus
● Cool conditions
● For beginners
● Easy to bloom

Crossandra infundibuliformis
(C. undulifolia)
(Firecracker flower)
● Intermediate conditions
● For everyone
● Easy to bloom

The crocus, long a favorite houseplant with its brilliant flowers, is a harbinger of spring, only 6in (15cm) tall. There are a variety of hybrids to brighten indoors with early spring color.

Give crocuses a bright exposure – a west or east window is fine. Plant the small corms as soon as you get them; put 6 or 8 corms in a 10in (25cm) pot filled with standard houseplant soil. Keep plants in a cool (50°F, 10°C) location out of the light until leaves are up 3–4in (7.5–10cm), then move them to a bright place. Keep the soil evenly moist; apply plant food after the leaves have formed and then again when plants are in bud. Allow plants to die back naturally and then store in a shady place – pot and all – for 6 to 8 weeks. After this rest repot in fresh soil.

To encourage bloom:
Give plenty of water when leaves are fully expanded. Keep plants cool (50°F, 10°C) until buds color.

A mass of orange flowers in springtime, *Crossandra* has shiny green leaves and grows to about 16in (40cm). Plants require little care. For a lavish display grow several plants in one container.

Grow at a sunny window, in equal parts of soil and humus. Keep evenly moist all year and feed every 2 weeks. Be sure plants have a good circulation of air – they do not respond in stagnant conditions. Even small plants bear handsome orange flowers and many times there is a second blooming at midsummer. New plants from seed started in spring or from stem cuttings.

To encourage bloom:
Be sure plants have good air circulation at all times.

42►

Cuphea ignea
(Cigar flower; firecracker flower; Mexican cigar plant)
● **Intermediate conditions**
● **For beginners**
● **Easy to bloom**

A shrubby plant up to 12in (30cm) tall, with bright red, black and white tubular flowers in the warm months. A pretty little pot plant for windows and easy to grow indoors.

Grow at a sunny window; use standard houseplant soil but be sure drainage is good. Keep soil evenly moist all year and provide good ventilation for plants. Feed every 2 weeks when in active growth. Spray with water occasionally to provide good humidity. Check plants for insects; mealy bugs attack sometimes – use appropriate remedies. Start new plants each year from seed in spring or from stem cuttings taken in summer.

To encourage bloom:
No special requirements. 44♦

Cyclamen
(Alpine violet; poor man's orchid; shooting star)
● **Cool conditions**
● **For a challenge**
● **Difficult to bloom**

Grown from a tuber, this is a charming plant up to 16in (40cm) tall, with flamboyant flowers in red, pink or white. The pretty heart shaped leaves are dark green or silver, and the single, double or fringed flowers start appearing in late winter.

Keep the cyclamen out of the sun – some shade is fine. Start the tubers, one to a 5in (12.5cm) pot, in late summer in a rich potting mix of equal parts of humus and soil. Set the top of the tuber slightly above the soil surface; otherwise, water may collect in the crown and cause rot. Keep the soil moist and the plants in coolness, 55–60°F (13–16°C): and feed every 2 weeks while in growth. When flowers fade in early spring, let the plants rest by gradually withholding water until the foliage dies. Keep nearly dry, the pot on its side in a shady place in coolness, until autumn. Then remove dead foliage and repot in fresh soil mix.

To encourage bloom:
Give plenty of water. Keep the plants cool and humid (but do not spray the flowers). Give resting period. 45♦

Cymbidium hybrids
- ● **Cool conditions**
- ● **For everyone**
- ● **Easy to bloom**

Here is a large group of grassy leaved orchids with magnificent flowers; a mature plant can have over 100 blooms. There are hundreds of hybrids and bloom can occur in any season depending upon the individual plant. Both standard and miniature varieties are available. Lovely accent for the indoor garden.

Cymbidiums needs a bright or sunny place – good light is essential for bloom. Use fir bark for potting and keep the medium quite moist all year. Do not feed. To make plants bloom, subject them to a cool period (55–60°F, 13–16°C) for about 6 weeks and then return to average home temperatures. Always provide good air circulation and adequate humidity (about 40 percent). Rarely bothered by insects. New plants from division of rhizome in spring.

To encourage bloom:
Provide cool period. Give as much sun as possible in autumn. 44♦

Dendrobium 'Gatton Sunray'
- ● **Warm conditions**
- ● **For everyone**
- ● **Easy to bloom**

A spectacular orchid hybrid growing to 48in (120cm) this cane type dendrobium has dark green leaves and masses of bright yellow and red flowers in summer – as many as 50 to a plant. Needs space but worth it – a truly lovely orchid for indoors.

Grow in sun. Pot in medium-grade fir bark kept evenly moist all year except in winter. Do not feed. Provide adequate humidity (30 percent) and good ventilation. After flowers fade allow plant to rest a little, with less moisture; when new growth starts, increase watering. Rarely bothered by insects. New plants from suppliers or division.

To encourage bloom:
Give plenty of sun. 47♦

59

Dipladenia splendens 'Rosea'
(Pink allamande)
- ● **Warm conditions**
- ● **For a challenge**
- ● **Difficult to bloom**

This climbs up to 15ft (4.6m) and has leathery leaves and fine pink flowers in summer – dozens to a plant. It can be pruned to be a small pot plant and will still flower. Ideal for basket growing and a beautiful addition to the indoor garden.

Grow at your sunniest window – without good sun it will not bloom. Pot in equal parts of soil and humus and be sure drainage is perfect. Water evenly while in growth; not so much the rest of the year. Feed every 2 weeks except when the plant is resting in winter. It is occasionally attacked by red spider mite; use appropriate remedies. Mist with water to provide the humidity essential for health. You can start new plants from stem cuttings or by sowing seed in spring.

To encourage bloom:
Provide ample sun. Keep slightly cooler (55–60°F, 13–16°C) in winter.

Echeveria 'Doris Taylor'
- ● **Warm conditions**
- ● **For beginners**
- ● **Easy to bloom**

A fine 20in (50cm) succulent with deep green spoon shaped leaves covered with white hairs. Flowers are red and yellow, borne in clusters from the center of the plant in spring. An attractive indoor plant.

Grow *Echeveria* at a sunny window – good light is essential for bloom. Use a potting mix of equal parts of sand and soil that drains readily. Water sparsely, allowing the soil to dry out between waterings. Feed monthly during warm weather. Do not get water on the leaves, as rot will result. Keep this plant in an airy position. New plants from seed, leaf cuttings or offsets in spring.

To encourage bloom:
Give plenty of sun. Keep cool in winter (45°F, 7°C). 46♦

Echinocereus baileyi
(Rainbow cactus)
- **Warm conditions**
- **For a challenge**
- **Difficult to bloom**

This is a small desert cactus that grows to about 8in (20cm) and requires little attention. It is light green in color and has spines. Flowers are a beautiful pink, and there are many to a plant in summer. This is a very good plant for growing under artificial lights.

Grow the rainbow cactus in your sunniest window – without good sun there will be sparse bloom. Use a potting mix of equal parts of sand and soil, and cover the top with some chipped gravel. Water and then allow to dry out before watering again. Feed every month except in winter, when plants like a 6 week rest with little water – move to a cooler location then if possible. Propagate by seed or offsets in spring.

To encourage bloom:
Give plenty of sun. Keep at 40°F (4°C) in winter. 46♦

Echinopsis hybrids
(Sea urchin cactus)
- **Warm conditions**
- **For beginners**
- **Easy to bloom**

Their beautiful large flowers make these cacti impossible to resist. They are breathtaking in summer in bloom. The body of the plant is dark green with spines and, depending on the particular hybrid, grows to 6–30in (15–75cm) in height. A lovely desert cactus for the home.

Grow at a sunny window. Use a potting medium of equal parts of sand and soil, and cover the top with some chipped gravel. Water freely in spring and summer, not so much the rest of the year. Feed every 2 weeks in warm weather. In winter move to a cool bright place and keep somewhat dry. Grow new plants from offsets in spring.

To encourage bloom:
Provide winter rest at 36°F (2°C) and keep rather dry.

Epidendrum cochleatum
(Clamshell; cockleshell orchid; shell flower)
● **Cool conditions**
● **For everyone**
● **Easy to bloom**

An amenable orchid up to 30in (75cm) tall, with light green leaves, and unusual shell shaped purple and yellow flowers in summer. Nice pot plant that blooms yearly with the minimum of care.

Grow the shell orchid in a bright location – a west or east window is fine. Use medium-grade fir bark for potting; water freely in warm months, not as much the rest of the year. Do not feed. Provide good ventilation. Rarely bothered by insects. Get new plants from suppliers.

To encourage bloom:
No special requirements. 47◗

Epiphyllum
(Epicactus; leaf cactus; orchid cactus)
● **Warm conditions**
● **For everyone**
● **Easy to bloom**

A cactus, but descended from the jungle dwellers, epiphyllums are generally large plants up to 30in (75cm) with dramatic 6–7in (15–18cm) flowers in red, pink, purple, yellow or white. Peak bloom season is midsummer and there are dozens of fine hybrids for windowsill beauty.

Grow in a bright window – an east or west exposure is fine, although epiphyllums need less light than other cacti. Use a potting mix of equal parts of small-grade fir bark and soil. Keep fairly moist during the growing period in the summer; the rest of the year, keep evenly moist. Feed with every other watering through the warm weather only. Plants are large and sprawling and need support – a small trellis is fine. Recently, miniature epiphyllums have been introduced, about 20in (50cm) high, and these make ideal houseplants. Take cuttings in spring for new plants.

To encourage bloom:
Observe the resting times. Keep at 50°F (10°C) during the winter.

Episcia cupreata
(Flame violet)
● **Intermediate conditions**
● **For everyone**
● **Easy to bloom**

This fine plant from the gesneriad family grows to 16in (40cm) with exquisite foliage – bright silver and green – and red flowers in early summer. It makes a fine hanging plant for indoor decoration.

Place episcias at a bright window but where they are protected from direct sun. Grow in a rich mix of equal parts of soil and humus. Water heavily during the growing times but be sure drainage is perfect. Provide humidity of 40 percent but do not mist leaves. Plants like warmth – about 70°(21°C),with a 5°F (3°C) drop in temperature at night. New plants can be grown from seeds, cuttings or offshoots.

To encourage bloom:
Provide adequate humidity. 48♦

Episcia dianthiflora
(Lace flower)
● **Intermediate conditions**
● **For everyone**
● **Easy to bloom**

This 14in (35cm) plant from the gesneriad group is a trailer with green velvety leaves and tufted white flowers. Bloom is in summer. Makes a very pretty show when grown as a basket plant.

This plant needs a bright but not sunny location. Grow in a mix of equal parts of soil and humus that drains readily. Plants are subject to rotting if overwatered. Use lime-free water. Provide suitable humidity of about 40 percent but do not mist foliage. Plants like warmth – about 70°F (21°C) during the day with a 5°F (3°C) drop in temperature at night. Propagate by rooting plantlets that develop on stolons.

To encourage bloom:
Provide adequate humidity. 48♦

Erica
(Heath)
- **Cool conditions**
- **For a challenge**
- **Difficult to bloom**

Heaths make lovely indoor plants, growing up to 24in (60cm), with narrow hard leaves and bell shaped or tubular flowers in clusters; they are generally summer blooming, although some winter-flowering species are popular. Many varieties and species. Fine outdoor plants that can make the transition into the home if given a little extra care.

Grow heaths and heathers in full sunlight – they need sun to bloom. Use a standard houseplant soil that drains well; never allow soil to become waterlogged and always use lime-free water. Feed moderately during warm months. For success with these plants grow cool (72°F, 22°C maximum) and be sure ventilation is good in the growing area – the plants succumb in a stagnant atmosphere. New plants from cuttings in spring.

To encourage bloom:
Give full sun.

Eucharis grandiflora
(Amazon lily)
- **Intermediate conditions**
- **For beginners**
- **Easy to bloom**

This fine amaryllis plant grows to 30in (75cm), and has large, shiny green leaves, and lovely glistening white flowers usually in spring and again in early autumn. A must for every indoor garden.

Grow the Amazon lily at a bright window but be sure there is protection from direct sun. Use a potting soil of equal parts of soil and humus, kept quite moist in early spring and late summer – the rest of the time it should be only slightly moist. Provide ample humidity (40 percent is fine). Feed moderately about once a month during growth, but not at all during resting times. Get new plants by division of clumps.

To encourage bloom:
Be sure to allow the plant to rest at proper times, with scanty water. 65♦

Above: **Eucharis grandiflora**
Bright white glistening flowers and
large dark green leaves combine to
display nature at her best. Highly
recommended for indoor gardens.
The blooms are fragrant. 64▶

65

Left: **Exacum affine**
Not spectacular but certainly worth space in the indoor garden, Exacum has small fragrant flowers that may last well into the winter months. 82♦

Right: **Euphorbia milii**
The stems of this small shrub are covered in sharp prickles. Bright red bracts give the plant appeal. 81♦

Below: **Euphorbia pulcherrima**
This popular indoor plant is tough to beat for midwinter color with its large showy bracts in shades of red, pink or white. This photograph shows several individual plants grouped together, each one of which produces bracts of a single color. The bracts do not change from white through pink to red as the plants become fully grown. 82♦

Above: **Fuchsia 'Snowcap'**
Lovely plants with pendent flowers in various colors, fuchsias can be difficult but worth the trouble. Highly regarded as an indoor plant where growing conditions are suitable. 83◆

Right: **Freesia**
Available in many different colors, the graceful flowers of freesias are exquisitely scented. Beautiful for indoor display as cut flowers. 83◆

Below: **Gardenia jasminoides**
Very popular but difficult to bloom, with lovely scented white flowers. 84◆

Above:
Gymnocalycium mihanovichi
Cultivars of the pretty globular cactus are available in a variety of colors, but without chlorophyll they cannot survive on their own. They are grafted onto a green rootstock. The original species (left) is green and will flower on its own roots. 85▶

Above right:
Gloriosa rothschildiana
A fine tuberous plant with narrow leaves and showy orange, crimson and yellow flowers in summer. Start the tubers in spring. 84▶

Right: **Guzmania lingulata 'Minor Orange'**
A fine small bromeliad, this guzmania has a rosette of apple green leaves. A spectacular orange inflorescence that lasts for several months puts this plant high on anyone's list for indoor color. 85▶

Above: **Heliotropium hybrid**
The fragrant purple flowers of heliotrope bloom from spring to autumn. A dependable plant for the beginner to grow with confidence. 87♦

Below: **Heliconia angustifolia**
Very tropical in appearance, with orange bracts and green-white flowers. Different, and one of the best heliconias for indoors. 87♦

Above: **Haemanthus katharinae**
Once coaxed into bloom, the
rewards are certainly worth the effort
– the bright red flower head will
certainly dazzle the eye. Needs
plenty of sun to thrive indoors. 86♦

Above: **Hibiscus rosa-sinensis**
Many varieties grow and bloom indoors, with large colorful flowers. Try in tubs in a garden room. 88♦

Left: **Hyacinthus orientalis**
The very fragrant packed flower spikes make hyacinths an indoor favorite. Varieties are available in many colors. Take your pick from white, yellow, pink or blue. 90♦

Above right: **Hoya bella**
This fine plant has waxy clusters of fragrant white-purple flowers that perfume a room. Especially rewarding in hanging baskets. 89♦

Right: **Hoya australis**
Blooming in summer or autumn, this plant from Australia has small white waxy flowers with a tinge of red around the center. Grow potbound. 89♦

75

Above: **Hypocyrta glabra**
*Known for their goldfish shaped
orange flowers, hypocyrtas are
compact plants; the shiny leaves of
this species make it handsome even
when not in bloom.* 91♦

Left: **Impatiens walleriana**
*One of the easiest houseplants to
grow, busy Lizzie produces red or
white flowers throughout the year.
Easy to propagate from cuttings.* 92♦

Right: **Hydrangea macrophylla
Lacecap type**
*Shrubby plants with fine clusters of
pink, blue or white flowers; a traditional
and very successful houseplant for
cool rooms.* 91♦

Above: **Ixia speciosa**
The rich crimson blooms of the corn lily provide dazzling indoor color in late spring. Very free-flowering, but it must be kept cool all the time. 92♦

Right: **Jacobinia carnea**
A handsome Brazilian plant with dark green leaves and plumes of pink flowers. Nice amenable plant for a sunny window. Easy to grow. 93♦

Above: **Ixora 'Peter Rapsley'**
An undemanding plant with upright growth and beautiful clusters of red flowers in early summer. A charming plant, not to be missed. 93♦

Above: **Kalanchoe pumila**
Here is a plant that can take almost any indoor situation and survive with beauty. Flowers are reddish purple, small leaves oval. 95♦

Above: **Kohleria amabilis**
*A gesneriad with lovely green leaves
and beautiful pink flowers in spring
and summer. Makes a fine show in a
hanging basket, but needs warm and
humid conditions to thrive.* 95♦

Euphorbia fulgens
(Scarlet plume)
● **Intermediate conditions**
● **For everyone**
● **Easy to bloom**

A fine shrub, up to 30in (75cm), with slender leaves. The tiny yellow flowers, borne in clusters, are surrounded by bright scarlet bracts and appear in winter. Some plants grow into handsome specimens for indoor decoration.

Grow the scarlet plume in full light – a west or east window is fine. Use a potting mix of equal parts of sand and soil. Water freely most of the year – only in winter should the soil be somewhat dry. Feed every 2 weeks in warm months, but not at all the rest of the year. Mealy bugs may attack the plant if it is grown without ample humidity: use appropriate remedies. Start new plants from cuttings taken in spring.

This plant is poisonous; the sap is irritant and should be washed off the skin immediately with cold water.

To encourage bloom:
Grow in good light.

Euphorbia milii
(Crown of thorns)
● **Intermediate conditions**
● **For everyone**
● **Easy to bloom**

Well known and well liked, this 30in (75cm) plant with dark green leaves bears small vivid red bracts surrounding insignificant flowers in winter. The stems have prickles, but the plant is very amenable to indoor culture, and worth its space.

Grow the crown of thorns in a bright sunny window. Pot in equal parts of standard houseplant soil and sand that is kept evenly moist all year except in winter and early spring, when a slight drying out is beneficial. Feed monthly in summer and autumn, but not at all the rest of the year. Plants resent drafts but like good air circulation. Take new plants from cuttings in spring.

This plant will exude a poisonous sap from cut surfaces and should be handled with gloves.

To encourage bloom:
Be sure this plant has a slight rest after blooming has finished. 67▶

81

Euphorbia pulcherrima
(Poinsettia)
- **Intermediate conditions**
- **For a challenge**
- **Difficult to bloom**

This highly prized indoor plant grows up to 30in (75cm). Leaves are scalloped and mossy green, and the 'flowers' are actually leafy bracts turning fiery red, white or pink.

The poinsettia needs a bright but not sunny location and intermediate temperatures about 65°F (18°C) or a little above. Grow in a rich porous houseplant soil. Drainage must be perfect. In winter, when the plant is in bloom, keep soil evenly moist. Reduce moisture when the leaves start to fall, and keep the plant cool.

In spring put the plant in the garden but leave it in its pot. Cut back and replace in fresh soil. In late summer bring the plant back into the house, and in autumn provide a period of uninterrupted darkness – at least 14 hours a day – to initiate flower buds for the winter. Get new plants from suppliers.

This plant is poisonous and should be handled with gloves.

To encourage bloom:
Keep humid and avoid drafts. Be sure a dark period is given – every day for at least 40 days. 66♦

Exacum affine
(Persian violet)
- **Cool conditions**
- **For everyone**
- **Easy to bloom**

Small fragrant violetlike flowers and shiny green leaves make this plant a beauty for indoors. New varieties grow up to 9in (23cm); older ones up to 18in (45cm). Plants can bloom from summer well into winter, when color is so needed at the windows. A real find.

Grow the Persian violet in full sun for healthy, robust plants. Use a potting soil of equal parts of humus and soil, and be sure drainage is perfect. Feed every 2 weeks when in active growth, and water evenly all year. Provide somewhat cool temperatures – about 60°F (16°C) – and good ventilation. Treat as an annual and raise new plants from seeds each year.

To encourage bloom:
No special requirements. 66♦

Freesia
- ● **Cool conditions**
- ● **For a challenge**
- ● **Difficult to bloom**

These fragrant flowering bulbs of the iris family are hardly easy to grow indoors, but not impossible. The trumpet-shaped flowers, 2in (5cm) long on stems up to 18in (45cm), come in many colors – white, yellow, pink, purple – and make excellent cut flowers for the living room.

Pot 6 corms, 1in (2.5cm) deep and 2in (5cm) apart, in a 6in (15cm) pot of two parts sandy loam, one part leafmold and one part old manure. Plant during the autumn for early spring bloom and give full light (no sun). Keep plants moist and cool, 60°F (16°C). Do not feed. After the flowers fade, gradually dry the soil, shake out the corms, and keep them dry for repotting in fresh mix for beautiful flowers next year.

To encourage bloom:
Ensure cool growing conditions. 69♦

Fuchsia
(Lady's eardrops)
- ● **Cool conditions**
- ● **For everyone**
- ● **Difficult to bloom**

These handsome plants, up to 36in (90cm) tall, bear pendent red, white, pink or purple flowers (or combinations of these colors) and dark green leaves. The plants are bushy, and excellent for hanging baskets or tubs.

Grow fuchsias in bright light but out of the sun, and keep the temperature between 55–60°F (13–16°C). Use a rich, well-drained potting soil of equal parts of humus and soil. Flower buds are set in spring and summer; feed every 2 weeks. Flood the plants while they are growing, and pinch at early stages to encourage branching. Mist foliage frequently and provide a buoyant atmosphere. Watch out for white fly. Take cuttings in winter for new plants. Difficult but worth the effort for their elegant display.

To encourage bloom:
Mist frequently; give plenty of water. Provide cool growing conditions and good ventilation. Give a cool period during the winter months at 45°F (7°C) with much less water. 68♦

Gardenia jasminoides
(Cape jasmine)
● **Warm conditions**
● **For a challenge**
● **Difficult to bloom**

These are evergreen shrubs up to about 30in (90cm) tall, with waxy dark green foliage and scented white flowers. They are well known and well loved, but difficult plants to achieve success with indoors, though not impossible. They are best suited to a conservatory or garden room.

Grow gardenias in bright light in summer and in a sunny place in winter. Use a well-drained, lime-free potting mix of equal parts of humus, soil and peat moss. Keep evenly moist with lime-free water. Be sure the plants have adequate humidity – about 40 percent. From spring to autumn, feed once a month with an acid fertilizer. Mist foliage frequently to avoid red spider infestations. Give a deep soaking in a sink or pail once a month. Buds may drop or fail to open if night temperature is above 70°F (21°C) or below 60°F (16°C). Propagate by cuttings in spring.

To encourage bloom:
Mist with tepid water frequently. Keep out of drafts and fluctuating temperatures, but always provide good ventilation for the plants. 68♦

Gloriosa rothschildiana
(Glory lily)
● **Intermediate conditions**
● **For beginners**
● **Easy to bloom**

This is a splendid tuberous plant of the lily family that grows to 6ft (1.8m) and has bright green foliage and exquisite 3in (7.5cm) orange and yellow flowers edged with crimson. Tubers started in very early spring bear flowers in midsummer that last for over a week. A showy plant, and easy to grow.

Grow the glory lily in sun – it likes heat. Use a loose potting mix of equal parts of houseplant soil and humus. Pot one tuber to a 5in (12.5cm) pot; set the tuber about 1in (2.5cm) below the surface of the soil; growth starts in a few days. Provide a bamboo stake or other support, as this is a climbing plant. Water heavily while in growth and feed every 2 weeks. When the flowers fade, let foliage die naturally; then store the plant in its pot in a cool dry place at 55° (13°C) for 6 to 9 weeks. Repot in fresh soil and start again.

To encourage bloom:
Give plenty of water. Observe the cool resting period. 71♦

Guzmania lingulata
(Orange star; scarlet star)
- ● Intermediate conditions
- ● For beginners
- ● Easy to bloom

A fine bromeliad growing to 30in (75cm), with apple green straplike leaves and star shaped inflorescence. The orange or scarlet bracts are impressive, but the flowers are insignificant in the center of the bracts. Bloom varies but generally occurs in summer.

Grow in sun or bright light – the more sun, the brighter the bracts. Use equal parts of fir bark and lime-free soil; do not firm the growing medium too much. Keep moderately moist all year with lime-free water and make sure the vase of the plant is filled with water from spring to autumn. Do not feed. Provide good ventilation and humidity of about 30 percent. Rarely bothered by insects. Grow new plants from offsets at the base of the mother plant; repot in bark and soil when 3–4in (7.5–10cm) high, usually in autumn or spring. Make sure the offsets are rooted before detaching them.

To encourage bloom:
Do not feed. Ensure warm and humid growing conditions. 71●

Gymnocalycium mihanovichi
- ● Warm conditions
- ● For everyone
- ● Easy to bloom

This is a 3in (7.5cm) globular cactus with pale yellow spines; it has abundant flowers in summer with outer petals varying in color from pink through red to purple and with a whitish center. This is a good houseplant that grows with little care.

Many varieties are available, including cultivars in which the body of the cactus is colored red, pink, yellow or black. These do not contain chlorophyll and must be grafted onto a green rootstock in order to survive; they will flower in ideal conditions.

Grow this cactus in sun. Use a medium of equal parts of soil and sand. Be sure the drainage is good. A thin layer of gravel on top will help to prevent crown rot if too much water is given. Water moderately all year except in winter, when the plant can be kept somewhat dry but never bone dry. Do not feed. New plants from seed. An easy plant to grow under artificial light.

To encourage bloom:
Observe winter dormant season at low temperature: 50°F (10°C). 70●

Haemanthus katharinae
(Blood flower; blood lily)
- **Cool conditions**
- **For a challenge**
- **Difficult to bloom**

This deciduous bulbous plant grows
to 16in (40cm), with bright green
leathery leaves. The plant bears a
salmon red sphere of small flowers
after the leaves have developed;
bloom timè is midsummer. Lovely,
but a bit temperamental.

Provide a sunny place for *H.
katharinae.* Pot one bulb to a 5in
(12.5cm) clay pot; use equal parts of
soil and sand. Leave the tip of the
bulb protruding. Water carefully –
very little moisture until the leaves
start to grow, then increase watering.
Do not feed. After flowering reduce
the moisture, but never let soil get
bone dry. Do not repot – instead
topdress the soil every year. Be alert
for crown rot if too much water
gathers at the base of the plant. New
plants from bulbs started in spring.

To encourage bloom:
Repot only every third year. 73▶

Hedychium gardnerianum
(Kahili ginger)
- **Warm conditions**
- **For a challenge**
- **Difficult to bloom**

A large tropical lily up to 6ft (1.8m)
tall, this plant has glossy green
canelike leaves, and bears exotic red
and yellow flowers in summer.
Grows like a weed once started.

Put this ginger at your sunniest
window – it needs lots of light. Grow
in large tubs – about 10in (25cm) in
diameter – in equal parts of sand,
humus and soil. Water heavily during
growth but reduce watering after the
plant blooms. Mist occasionally with
tepid water. Excellent terrace or patio
plant where climatic conditions
allow. Protect from cold in winter.
New plants from rhizomes in spring.

To encourage bloom:
Give plenty of sun and water.

Heliconia angustifolia
- Warm conditions
- For a challenge
- Difficult to bloom

This member of the banana family is large, growing to 60in (1.5m) so you will need adequate space to grow it. The plant has big glossy green leaves and showy flower bracts, orange-red, edges lined green. Flowers are dramatic and appear in summer.

H. angustifolia needs a sunny window. Pot in equal parts of soil and humus and be sure drainage is good. Water heavily in summer but reduce watering in winter, when plants should be allowed to rest with less moisture and in coolness (about 55°F, 13°C). Feed every two weeks during growth and spray plant with tepid water in warm months; these plants require excellent humidity. Difficult but not impossible to bloom, and plants make handsome accents for patio or terrace where the climate allows. Propagate by dividing rootstock when growth starts in spring.

To encourage bloom:
Provide warmth: 75°F (24°C) and ensure position in full sun. 72♦

Heliotropium hybrids
(Cherry pie; heliotrope)
- Intermediate conditions
- For beginners
- Easy to bloom

Heliotrope is an old favorite, a 30in (75cm) plant, with oval wrinkled dull green leaves, and clusters of fragrant blue-purple flowers that open from spring to autumn. As pot plants they are best raised annually or every second year, because they get straggly (although they can be pruned hard in early spring with success). A plant that gives a nice touch of outdoors for indoors.

Grow heliotrope at a bright window a west or east exposure is fine. Use equal parts of humus and soil for potting, and water copiously. These are thirsty plants. Feed every 2 weeks during growth. They can tolerate coldness (45°F, 7°C) if necessary and are rarely bothered by insects in the home. New plants from seed or stem cuttings in spring.

To encourage bloom:
Water freely while in growth. Rest in winter and provide good ventilation during the summer months. 72♦

Hibiscus rosa-sinensis

(Chinese hibiscus; Chinese rose; rose mallow)

● **Warm conditions**
● **For everyone**
● **Easy to bloom**

A large 48in (120cm) free-flowering plant, hibiscus grows well in tubs in a porch or garden room. Plants have lush green foliage and bear mammoth, paper-thin, red, pink, orange, white or yellow flowers that each last only a few days, followed by more flowers – bloom continues for about 6 weeks in midsummer.

Sun is the key to success with hibiscus so put them at your sunniest window. Grow in equal parts of soil and sand, and be sure drainage is perfect. Flood with water during growth; these are thirsty plants. Feed every 2 weeks. Spray foliage with tepid water. Prune back small specimens to 4in (10cm) in early spring; large plants by one third. Watch for spider mites, which like these plants. Propagate by taking cuttings in spring.

To encourage bloom:
Provide ample sun and water. Drafts and fluctuating temperatures may cause the buds to drop before opening. Rest the plant during the winter at 50°F (10°C). 74♦

Hippeastrum hybrids

(Amaryllis)

● **Intermediate conditions**
● **For beginners**
● **Easy to bloom**

These striking bulbous plants with strap foliage bear large flowers in many colors; the stalks are up to 26in (65cm) long. A colorful display in early spring.

Buy good quality bulbs in autumn and start in growth during the winter; use one bulb to a 6–7in (15–18cm) clay pot; allow 1in (2.5cm) space between the walls and the bulb. Let the upper third of the bulb extend above the soil line. Use any standard houseplant soil. Set the pot in a cool shady place and grow almost dry until the flower bud is 6in (15cm) tall. Then move the pot into a sunny window and water heavily.

After the plant blooms, keep it growing so the leaves can make food for next year's flowers. When foliage browns let the soil go dry for about 10 to 12 weeks or until you see new flower buds emerging; then replant in fresh soil. Propagate by seeds or by removing offsets when repotting.

To encourage bloom:
Feed after flowering until the leaves die down. Observe the rest period.

Hoya australis
(Porcelain flower; wax plant; wax vine)
● **Intermediate conditions**
● **For a challenge**
● **Difficult to bloom**

This robust 30in (75cm) plant from Australia has shiny green leaves, and clusters of small white waxy flowers in summer or autumn. This species is somewhat easier to grow than the old-fashioned *Hoya carnosa*. It is best grown in a hanging container.

Grow the porcelain flower in a sunny place. Use a potting soil of equal parts of soil and humus; drainage must be perfect. Water heavily during warm months but never allow soil to become soggy. In autumn and winter allow to dry out between waterings. Feed every 2 weeks in summer. The plant blooms off old wood so do not prune. Repot only when necessary; the roots resent disturbance. Topdress every few months using fresh soil. New plants can be grown from cuttings taken in spring or autumn.

To encourage bloom:
Do not overwater. Keep cool in winter at 50°F (10°C). 75♦

Hoya bella
(Miniature wax plant)
● **Intermediate conditions**
● **For a challenge**
● **Difficult to bloom**

This 12–24in (30–60cm) vining plant resembles its larger cousin *Hoya carnosa*. It is excellent for small window gardens and hanging baskets. Leaves are small and dark green, and it has waxy purple-centered white fragrant blooms.

Grow the miniature wax plant in bright light. Use a well-drained potting soil of equal parts of humus and houseplant soil. Grow in small pots for best results. Give plenty of water in spring, summer, and autumn; in winter let the soil go almost dry. Feed monthly during warm weather. Mist the foliage frequently and check for mealy bugs, which adore wax plants. Do not remove stems on which flowers have been produced; they are also the source of next season's bloom. Propagate by cuttings in spring.

To encourage bloom:
Grow in small well-drained clay pots; crushed brick can be added. Do not prune or move the plant once in bud. Keep cooler (55°F, 13°C) during winter months. 75♦

Hoya carnosa
(Wax plant)
- **Intermediate conditions**
- **For a challenge**
- **Difficult to bloom**

These attractive vines, with leathery leaves and charming clusters of fragrant white flowers, are old favorites. They can reach up to 20ft (6m), and make magnificent showy plants for summer bloom. Only mature plants are likely to bloom; young ones (2 years or under) seldom do. Best grown on a trellis or support, but is also handsome in hanging baskets.

Grow in bright light; use a standard houseplant soil and grow potbound. Give plenty of water during growth but in winter let the soil go almost dry. Do not remove the stem or spur on which flowers have been produced – this is the source of next year's bloom. Do not feed. Mist foliage frequently to ward off mealy bugs. Propagate by taking stem cuttings in spring.

To encourage bloom:
Buy mature plants. Do not prune at all – this will check flowering. Maintain good light as buds form.

Hyacinthus orientalis
(Hyacinth)
- **Cool conditions**
- **For beginners**
- **Easy to bloom**

Erect bulbous plants with 10in (25cm) stems, hyacinths have long narrow leaves. Flower spikes are closely packed with waxy, very fragrant flowers available in shades of red, blue, yellow and white. Can be forced to bloom in spring or winter but only once – then they should be planted outside. Many varieties are available.

Grow at a bright window – sun is not necessary. Use a potting mix of equal parts of soil and humus that drains readily. Water freely when the plant is growing. Be careful to keep cool (50°F, 10°C) and in a dark place until growth is under way, then bring out into the light. Rest for 8 weeks after flowering; leave in the pot in a cool (50°F, 10°C) place. Do not feed. Grow new plants from offsets. Can also be grown over water.

To encourage bloom:
The cool, dark period of 8–10 weeks after the bulbs have been potted is vital for forcing bulbs for the winter; without it the plants will not make sufficient root to support flowers. 74♦

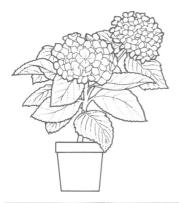

Hydrangea macrophylla
(Common hydrangea; house hydrangea; snowball flower)
● **Cool conditions**
● **For beginners**
● **Easy to bloom**

Hydrangeas are large-leaved shrubs with showy clusters of white, blue or pink flowers. They are bushy, grow to about 24in (60cm) and bloom in spring and summer.

Grow in sun; use a rich potting mix of equal parts of soil and humus. Water freely when in growth and feed every 2 weeks. Keep cool (65 °F, 18°C), and be sure there is good circulation of air. After plants bloom, cut back shoots to 2 joints; repot in slightly acid soil and set outdoors; feed and keep the soil moist.

After the first frost, store indoors in a shady, cool place, and water once a month. In early spring increase warmth, light and water. When the plant is actively growing, move to a window. The degree of soil acidity determines the coloring of the pink and blue varieties. A pink plant can be made blue by changing the soil to an acid pH 5.5. New plants from suppliers or take stem cuttings.

To encourage bloom:
Observe cool growing conditions and winter rest period. 77♦

Hypocyrta glabra
● **Intermediate conditions**
● **For everyone**
● **Easy to bloom**

This very popular 15in (38cm) plant, ideal for indoor growing, has small leathery bright green leaves, and fascinating orange flowers in summer. Very easy to grow, this pleasing little plant adds a touch of the unusual to the indoor garden. Not to be missed.

Grow in a bright but not sunny window all year except in winter, when some sun is necessary. Use equal parts of small-grade fir bark and soil. Water, allow to dry out, and water again. Feed every 2 weeks except after bloom; then allow to rest a few months with no feeding. After bloom, pinch back plants by about 4in (10cm) to encourage new growth. Provide additional misting in summer. Grow new plants from tip cuttings in spring.

To encourage bloom:
Provide good sun in winter. 76♦

91

Impatiens walleriana
(Busy Lizzie; patience plant; patient Lucy; snap weed; sultana; touch-me-not)
● **Intermediate conditions**
● **For beginners**
● **Easy to bloom**

This shrubby plant grows to 24in (60cm) and is an excellent indoor subject. Leaves are dark green and flowers generally in shades of red, also white. Many hybrids are available. Flowers appear on and off throughout the year, and first begin to open in midsummer.

Grow in a bright window, but sun is not needed. Use a loose houseplant soil – drainage must be perfect or plants suffer. Water heavily during growth (allowing soil to dry out between waterings), but keep barely moist in winter and move to a cool place, 60°F (16°C). After blooming, cut back the plant to about 4in (10cm) and topdress with soil and grow on again. Propagate by taking cuttings or sowing seed in spring.

To encourage bloom:
Do not pamper – allow soil to dry out between waterings. Young plants often produce the most flowers – keep a supply of young plants coming along from cuttings. 76♦

Ixia speciosa
(Corn lily; grass lily)
● **Cool conditions**
● **For a challenge**
● **Difficult to bloom**

This bulbous plant is lovely, with grassy green foliage up to 24in (60cm), and large clusters of deep crimson flowers in late spring; hybrids extend the color range into white, cream, yellow, blue, and purple. Generally an outdoor plant, it does well in pots and makes a colorful statement at the window.

Grow at a west or east window; use a potting mix that drains well – standard houseplant soil is fine. Plants do best in small clay pots, 4–5in (10–12.5cm), planting 2 corms to a pot. Water sparsely at first, but when foliage starts to grow increase the watering. Do not feed. After it blooms, allow the plant to die back naturally; store in a cool dry place for 8 to 10 weeks. Repot in fresh soil. A truly handsome plant, and the flowers are excellent for cutting.

To encourage bloom:
Observe resting time and grow in cool conditions (50°F, 10°C). 78♦

Ixora coccinea
(Flame of the woods; Indian jasmine)
● **Cool conditions**
● **For beginners**
● **Easy to bloom**

This robust houseplant grows to 30in (75cm), and has bright green rounded leaves, and clusters of brilliant red flowers in early summer. Easy to grow and very rewarding, as even young plants will bloom.

Grow in sun. Use a potting mix of equal parts of lime-free soil and humus. Keep quite moist during growth but barely wet in winter. Feed every 2 weeks during growth. Group several plants together for a lovely show. Some plants bloom on and off throughout the year if conditions are good. Prefers a cool environment – 60°F (16°C). Outstanding hybrids include *Ixora* 'Super King' and 'Peter Rapsley'. Start new plants from cuttings taken in spring.

To encourage bloom:
Give plenty of sun and humidity. Do not move plants; buds may drop. 79♦

Jacobinia carnea
(Brazilian plume; king's crown)
● **Intermediate conditions**
● **For everyone**
● **Easy to bloom**

This 30in (75cm) plant from Brazil has downy green leaves, and plumes of pink flowers that last a few days. Hardly a spectacular plant, but pleasing for the indoor garden if you have extra space.

Grow in a sunny window. Pot in standard houseplant soil. Keep evenly moist all year; feed every 2 weeks. Plants suffer from lack of water, so keep well watered. Ventilate when the temperature exceeds 70°F (21°C). Most plants last only a year or so and then decline. Take tip cuttings in spring for new plants; discard the old ones.

To encourage bloom:
Provide plenty of sun. 79♦

Jasminum polyanthum
(Pink jasmine)
- **Intermediate conditions**
- **For everyone**
- **Easy to bloom**

This beautifully fragrant jasmine has mid-green leaves and white and pale pink flowers from autumn to spring. Plants climb to 10ft (3m) or more and need support. This is a good offbeat plant for the indoor garden.

Grow jasmine in sun – otherwise it will not do well and will not flower. Use a rich potting mix of equal parts of humus and soil. Feed with acid fertilizer every month during growth. Mist foliage occasionally and give pots a deep soaking in the sink once a month. Provide ample humidity (50 percent). Repot every second year. New plants from cuttings in spring.

To encourage bloom:
Provide ample sun and very good ventilation. Keep cooler in winter (55°F, 13°C) during flowering.

Kalanchoe blossfeldiana
(Flaming Katy; Tom Thumb)
- **Intermediate conditions**
- **For beginners**
- **Easy to bloom**

This 12in (30cm) succulent has leathery green leaves, and bright red flowers in winter, making it especially appealing. Bloom sometimes occurs again in spring. Hybrids are available with pink, white or yellow flowers.

Grow at a bright window, but sunlight can scorch this plant. Use a standard houseplant soil – add one cup of sand to a 6in (15cm) pot. Do not feed. Allow soil to dry out between waterings. Do not mist plants, as the succulent leaves will be harmed. Any water on the base of the plant or foliage can cause rot. Provide good ventilation. Trim back bottom leaves when they become too thick. Repot every second year. New plants from seed in spring or stem cuttings in summer.

To encourage bloom:
Do not overwater at any time, but especially in winter.

Kalanchoe pumila
- **Intermediate conditions**
- **For beginners**
- **Easy to bloom**

This dwarf plant, up to 6in (15cm) high, is valued for its winter blooming red-purple flowers. The leaves are gray with a waxy bloom. It is a good basket plant.

Grow in bright light – sun is not needed. Use a potting mix of equal parts of sand and soil, and be sure drainage is good. Water freely during most of the year except in winter, when watering can be tapered off slightly. Do not feed. Avoid getting water on the fleshy leaves, or they might rot. New plants from cuttings in summer or seeds in spring.

To encourage bloom:
Give plenty of light. 79♦

Kohleria amabilis
(Tree gloxinia)
- **Warm conditions**
- **For a challenge**
- **Difficult to bloom**

This fine 16in (40cm) gesneriad has bright green leaves, and pink flowers in spring and summer. It is best grown in a hanging basket, where it makes a lovely show.

Grow in bright light, but sun is not necessary. Use a rich soil mix of equal parts of humus and soil. Drainage must be good. Water heavily during growth, much less the rest of the time – about once a week – but never allow the soil to become bone dry. Do not mist plants, as this can rot the hairy leaves. Take tip cuttings for new plants, or large rhizomes may be separated and single scales planted like seeds.

To encourage bloom:
Grow warm and humid. Provide cooler conditions during the winter resting period at 55°F (13°C). 80♦

Laelia anceps
- **Intermediate conditions**
- **For everyone**
- **Easy to bloom**

This is a showy orchid, with leathery leaves, and fine 4in (10cm) fragrant pink flowers in summer or autumn. It makes a handsome plant and the flowers last for weeks. It is generally an amenable houseplant, a sterling orchid for the beginner, and sure to please in any indoor garden.

Grow in full sun, as it needs really good light. Use a potting mix of medium-grade fir bark. Keep moist all year. Do not feed, but mist this plant with tepid water to promote good humidity. Repot only every third year. Rarely bothered by insects – leaves are too tough. Buy new plants from specialists or divide mature plants (with over 7 growths).

To encourage bloom:
Give plenty of sun, and a winter resting period with slightly cooler and drier conditions. 97♦

Lantana camara
(Common lantana; shrub verbena; yellow sage)
- **Intermediate conditions**
- **For everyone**
- **Difficult to bloom**

This is a colorful pot plant up to 36in (90cm) with oval wrinkled leaves and many 2in (5cm) wide flat clusters of yellow and orange flowers in spring and summer. Many hybrids are available with white, pink, or red flowers. A good accent plant in the indoor garden.

Grow on a sunny windowsill– it needs direct light to bloom. Pot in standard packaged soil. Water evenly throughout the year but never allow the soil to become soggy. Feed every 2 weeks in warm months, not at all the rest of the year. Propagate from cuttings or seed in spring.

To encourage bloom:
Grow in sun. Observe a winter rest period at 50°F (10°C). 98♦

Above: **Laelia anceps**
A large orchid but well worth its space; bears 4in (10cm) pink flowers that last for two months or more on the plant. Very showy in bloom. Needs plenty of sun to thrive. 96\blacktriangleright

Above: **Lilium auratum**
What could be nicer than these fine large white lilies in the home? In pots they add a colorful note to the window garden in summer. 113♦

Below: **Lantana camara**
Lantanas make fine indoor plants, with their yellow and orange flowers and rather odd wrinkled leaves. Good for your brightest window. 96♦

Above: **Lapageria rosea**
The beautiful flowers of this vining plant – here the red with the white-flowered variety – make a stunning show in summer and autumn. Excellent if you have room. 113▸

Above: **Lobivia aurea**
This cactus is not difficult to bloom indoors, and bears colorful, though short-lived, yellow flowers. 114♦

Above right: **Lycaste aromatica**
This popular small orchid with perky yellow flowers is an excellent plant for those new to orchid growing. 115♦

Right: **Mammillaria zeilmanniana**
White and brick red spines decorate this cactus, and flowers are violet-red. Very showy. Ideal for beginners; easy to propagate. 115♦

Above: **Masdevallia coccinea**
Beautiful flowers shaped like kites make this plant look very unlike the orchid it is. Handsome foliage; certainly worth space in cool situations. Provides welcome winter color. 116▸

Above: **Medinilla magnifica**
And magnificent it is in bloom, with pendulous panicles of carmine flowers in pink bracts. 117♦

Below: **Miltonia 'Peach Blossom'**
A fine small orchid with flat-faced pink flowers, large for the size of the plant. A popular variety. 117♦

Above: **Nerine bowdenii**
This bulbous plant produces a welcome display of attractive pink flowers in autumn. 119♦

Above left: **Miltonia roezlii**
An easy orchid to grow in most situations, this miltonia has white flowers tinged with purple, which last many weeks on the plant. 118♦

Left: **Nerium oleander**
Bushy and big but colorful, with pink, white or red flowers at intervals throughout the summer. 119♦

Right: **Narcissus tazetta 'Paper White'**
Even the novice gardener can bring this lovely white-flowering plant into bloom indoors. Fragrant. 118♦

Above: **Notocactus leninghausii**
A very pretty cactus with soft yellowish spines and bright yellow flowers. Only mature plants bloom. Withstands negligence. 120♦

Left: **Notocactus ottonis**
Very easy to grow and a splendid sight in bloom. It produces many offsets, making propagation simple. Young plants will flower. 120♦

Right: **Odontioda Jumbo 'Mont Millais'**
One of the brilliantly colored hybrids of Odontoglossum and Cochlioda. A stunning indoor plant. 121♦

Above: Passiflora caerulea
*Known for its spectacular 3in
(7.5cm) flowers of white, blue, and
purple, here is nature at her best. A
large vine that needs space.* 124♦

Left: Pachystachys lutea
*A shrubby plant with lance shaped
leaves and clearly marked veins;
overlapping yellow bracts protect the
white tubular flowers.*123♦

Right: Odontoglossum grande
*A most dependable orchid, with
large yellow and brown flowers that
last for weeks. Sure to bloom.* 121♦

Above: **Pelargonium zonale**
Compact clusters of single or double blooms above ring-marked leaves signify these classic geraniums. Ideal for beginners. 125♦

Below: **Pelargonium peltatum 'Rouletti'**
A new bicolored hybrid. Trailing geraniums, ideal for hanging baskets, prefer a little shade. 125♦

Above: **Pelargonium grandiflorum 'Fanny Eden'**
Large, multicolored flowers make these hybrids a particular favorite. Like most pelargoniums, they thrive in bright but cool conditions. 125♦

Above: **Pentas lanceolata**
*Showy umbels of pink flowers make
Pentas a great beauty. A compact
and amenable houseplant.* 126♦

Left: **Pleione formosana
'Snow White'**
*Can't grow anything? Try this
exquisite white flowering orchid from
China. Sure to please – with lovely
4in (10cm) blooms in spring.* 127♦

Lapageria rosea
(Copihue; Chilean bellflower)
- ● **Cool conditions**
- ● **For a challenge**
- ● **Difficult to bloom**

A vining plant to 10ft (3m) with leathery dark green leaves and handsome funnel shaped crimson flowers spotted white inside. A white-flowered variety is also available. Plants bloom on and off through summer and autumn, and make quite a sight at the window. Can tolerate abuse if necessary and still bloom. Excellent indoor plant.

Grow in shade; too much sun will burn the leaves. Use a rich lime-free potting mix of equal parts of humus and houseplant soil. Keep quite moist with lime-free water in spring, summer and autumn. In winter allow the plant to rest. Provide suitable support, such as a trellis. Feed moderately, about 4 times a year. These robust plants bloom best in the second year in new conditions. Get new plants from seed or by layering shoots in spring.

To encourage bloom:
Grow plants in small pots. 99◗

Lilium auratum
(Golden-rayed lily)
- ● **Cool conditions**
- ● **For a challenge**
- ● **Difficult to bloom**

These showy bulbous plants, up to 48in (120cm) tall, have trumpet-shaped fragrant white flowers striped with gold, and strap shaped leaves. Many hybrids have been developed and most are excellent in the home. Fine cut flowers.

Pot the bulbs in equal parts of humus and lime-free soil in autumn and keep cool (50–60°F, 10–16°C) until growth is 4in (10cm) high. Then move to bright light and slightly warmer conditions; keep the medium moist until flowering time and leaves start to yellow; then keep just moist with lime-free water in cool conditions (55°F, 13°C) until autumn. Do not feed. Provide ample air circulation. Repot bulbs each year in fresh potting soil.

To encourage bloom:
Start in shade and coolness. Be sure to plant the bulb at least 5in (12.5cm) deep; this lily develops secondary roots from the stem that feed and maintain the flowers. 98◗

Lithops
(Living stones; pebble plant; stone face)
- **Warm conditions**
- **For a challenge**
- **Difficult to bloom**

Lithops is a genus of 50 succulent plants from South Africa that resemble small stones. Most grow no more than a few inches tall and have fleshy leaves. Daisy-like white or yellow flowers appear in autumn. Unusual. For a good display grow several plants together. There are many species and varieties.

These plants need the sunniest window you have. Grow in equal parts of sand, soil and gravel. Water just enough to keep the medium barely moist, but never soggy; plants die quickly if watered too much. Do not feed. Grow warm; use small pots. Plants appreciate an area with good air circulation Get new plants by sowing seed in spring.

To encourage bloom:
Give ample sun; do not overwater. Rest throughout the winter at 40°F (4°C) with no water at all.

Lobivia aurea
(Golden lily cactus)
- **Warm conditions**
- **For everyone**
- **Easy to bloom**

This globular cactus is about 4in (10cm) tall with closely ribbed dark green stems and light brown spines. Lovely golden-yellow flowers open to 2in (5cm) across in summer. A fine indoor plant.

Grow this cactus in your sunniest spot. Pot in equal parts of sand and soil. Water freely during the summer months. Be sure drainage is good. Do not feed. Do not get water on the plant, or rot may result. It can be depended upon to bloom if given sufficient sun and less water in winter. Grow new plants from offsets or seed in spring. Dry offsets for a few days if not already rooted.

To encourage bloom:
Observe winter rest time at a temperature of 40°F (4°C). 100♦

Lycaste aromatica
(Cinnamon orchid)
- **Intermediate conditions**
- **For everyone**
- **Easy to bloom**

This charming 14in (35cm) orchid from Mexico is ideal for home growing, taking little space. The 2in (5cm) yellow scented flowers stay fresh for three weeks. Leaves are semideciduous and papery thin. A mature plant bears as many as 30 flowers in early spring.

Grow the cinnamon orchid at a bright window, but sun is not necessary. Use medium-grade fir bark as a potting mix, and a 5–6in (12.5–15cm) clay pot is fine for the container. Keep the mix evenly moist all year except in winter, when little water should be given until flower buds show: then increase watering. Rest severely with only scant moisture after bloom, until you see new growth starting, and then resume watering. Do not feed. Repot only when absolutely necessary – this plant hates to be disturbed. Provide good humidity (about 40 percent) and maintain good air circulation. Rarely bothered by insects. New plants by division.

To encourage bloom:
Observe resting times. 101♦

Mammillaria zeilmanniana
(Rose pin cushion)
- **Warm conditions**
- **For beginners**
- **Easy to bloom**

A 4in (10cm) diameter globular cactus, this fine plant bears violet flowers in summer. Not difficult to coax into bloom if given a cold period in winter, after which even small plants will bloom. Nice indoor accent for limited space.

This cactus needs sun and plenty of it – place it in a sunny window. Pot in equal parts of soil and sand and dress the top with chipped gravel. Water moderately in summer and do not feed. Likes a buoyant atmosphere and requires artificial light in autumn to bear flowers. In winter rest it in cool conditions with little water. Grow new plants from offsets freely produced in spring.

To encourage bloom:
Give plenty of sun and keep cool (40°F,4°C) and almost dry throughout the winter. 101♦

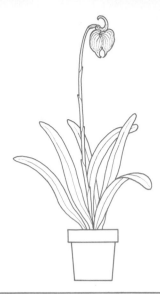

Manettia bicolor
(Candy corn plant; firecracker plant; firecracker vine)
- **Intermediate conditions**
- **For beginners**
- **Easy to bloom**

This vining plant, which with pruning can be kept to 40in (1m) tall, has narrow shiny green leaves, and bright scarlet tubular flowers tipped with yellow from late spring to autumn. A nice plant if you have space for it.

Grow the firecracker plant in a fairly shady place. Use standard packaged houseplant soil. Water freely all year but do not let the soil get soggy. Feed every 2 weeks during warm months. Use a small trellis support to train the plant. Mist occasionally with tepid water to maintain good humidity. Grow new plants from cuttings taken in spring.

To encourage bloom:
Give plenty of water when growing.

Masdevallia coccinea
- **Cool conditions**
- **For everyone**
- **Easy to bloom**

One of the famous cool growing orchids, this is a showy plant in winter with its 2in (5cm) scarlet flowers. Leaves are dark green and straplike, and grow to about 12in (30cm). A true beauty of nature.

This plant likes a shady place in an airy situation. Plant in small-grade fir bark. Keep evenly moist all year – do not allow to dry out. Use clay pots. Provide ample humidity (about 40 percent) and mist plants with tepid water in warm weather. Do not feed. Repot every third year but use the same small pot: overpotting results in sparse flowering. Never bothered by insects but occasionally, if grown too damp, leaf rot may result. Must have ample ventilation to thrive. Get new plants by division in spring.

To encourage bloom:
Grow in small pots, 3–4in (7.5-10cm) for best results. 102◗

Medinilla magnifica
(Love plant; rose grape)
● Intermediate conditions
● For a challenge
● Difficult to bloom

This lush green-blue leafy plant, up to 40in (1m) tall, has pendulous panicles of carmine flowers in pink bracts, generally in spring but blossoming can also occur in late summer. Only recently available from suppliers, the love plant is showy and worth its space at a window. A real display of color.

This plant likes a very bright spot at your window, but sun is not necessary. Use a potting mix of equal parts of soil and humus that drains rapidly: stagnant soil can ruin the plant. Keep soil evenly moist except in winter, when it should be barely moist but never bone dry. Give a winter rest period at 60°F (16°C). Feed every 2 weeks when in growth. Provide ample humidity, as this plant likes moisture in the air. Rarely bothered by insects. Propagate by cuttings or buy young plants from suppliers.

To encourage bloom:
Keep in humid conditions. Only mature plants will bloom. 103♦

Miltonia 'Peach Blossom'
(Pansy orchid)
● Cool conditions
● For everyone
● Easy to bloom

Growing to 12in (30cm), this fine small plant has grassy leaves and lovely flat-faced 2in (5cm) pink flowers, several to a stem. Bloom is generally in autumn, but the plant may bear flowers in summer some years. Many *Miltonia* hybrids are available. They make excellent pot plants for the indoor garden.

This plant likes a bright but not sunny location where there is excellent ventilation – it does not thrive in a stagnant place. Grow in medium-grade fir bark kept moist all year, and spray the growing area with tepid water to maintain humidity of not less than 40 percent. Do not feed. Dry out slightly after flowering but never allow the fir bark to become bone dry. Rarely bothered by insects, this is generally a most amenable plant. Get new plants from suppliers or by division.

To encourage bloom:
Grow in a well-ventilated and bright place. Provide humidity. 103♦

Miltonia roezlii
(Pansy orchid)
● **Intermediate conditions**
● **For everyone**
● **Easy to bloom**

A 12in (30cm) orchid with blue-green leaves, this plant bears pansy shaped white flowers tinged with purple in autumn. It is very pretty, and takes up little space, making it ideal for windows. A gem not to be missed for dependable bloom.

Grow this orchid at a west window – some sun is needed but no direct rays. Pot in medium-grade fir bark; be sure drainage is good. Water thoroughly and then allow to dry out before watering again. Do not feed. Keep cooler and drier in winter. Rarely bothered by insects. Get new plants from suppliers or division.

To encourage bloom:
Allow to dry out a little in winter in a cool place (50°F, 10°C). 104♦

Narcissus tazetta 'Paper White'
● **Cool conditions**
● **For beginners**
● **Easy to bloom**

Nothing is as pretty as these winter flowering beauties to liven a room. Plants grow to 20in (50cm) tall from bulbs, and the flowers are sweetly scented. In handsome trays, they make an ideal room decoration. Very easy to grow.

Grow in gravel, bulb fiber or soil in autumn, in shallow bowls. Plant bulbs with tips showing. Water little at first and keep in a dark, cool place at 50°F (10°C). When leaves are 4in (10cm) high move to bright light and warmer conditions. Keep the medium uniformly moist at all times. After blooming, the plants are discarded. Other cultivars are available in different colors and all are handsome to grow.

To encourage bloom:
Start in a cool, shady place, then move to light and warmer conditions after 6 to 8 weeks. Do not allow to dry out while they are growing. 105♦

Nerine bowdenii
- ● Cool conditions
- ● For beginners
- ● Easy to bloom

This beautiful South African bulbous plant reaches 20in (50cm), and has soft pink flowers in the autumn, blooming before foliage starts to grow. Flowers are exotic, several to a cluster, and last several days. Very pretty for that unusual touch indoors.

This plant needs a sunny location; start bulbs in late summer using equal parts of sand and soil. Grow one bulb to a 5in (12.5cm) pot. Water sparsely at first and increase watering as flowers appear and then as leaves mature. Do not feed. Provide good humidity (40 percent) and an airy place for the plant. Allow foliage to ripen naturally and then reduce water somewhat for several months. Repot in fresh soil mix.

To encourage bloom:
Observe summer resting time. 105♦

Nerium oleander
(Oleander; rose bay)
- ● Intermediate conditions
- ● For everyone
- ● Difficult to bloom

Growing to 40in (1m), this leafy plant bears fine pink flowers on and off throughout the summer. Forms with lovely white or red flowers are also available. Mature plants are best and generally require little care. Take care when handling the plant, it is extremely poisonous.

Grow oleanders at your sunniest window, because they like heat. Use a potting mix of equal parts of soil and humus. A thirsty plant, the oleander needs plenty of tepid water all year except in winter, when soil should be slightly damp. Feed every other watering. Repot yearly in fresh soil. During the autumn cut back the plant to about 10in (25cm), and move to a cooler place at 50 °F (10 °C). Grow new plants from stem cuttings taken in spring or autumn.

To encourage bloom:
Give plenty of water; always tepid. Keep warm and sunny with maximum ventilation in summer. 104♦

Notocactus leninghausii
- ● **Warm conditions**
- ● **For everyone**
- ● **Difficult to bloom**

Growing to 5in (12.5cm) across and up to 36in (90cm) tall, this fine desert cactus bears lovely yellow flowers in summer. It makes a very suitable indoor subject and lives for years with minimum care.

Grow this cactus at a sunny window. Pot in equal parts of sand and soil, and dress the surface with chipped gravel. Water freely in midsummer, not so much the rest of the year. Do not feed. It is rarely attacked by insects. In winter rest the plant in a cool (50°F, 10°C) place with little water but where there is sun. Return it to the window in early spring, and resume watering. Grow new plants from offsets or from seed; start both in spring.

To encourage bloom:
Provide ample sun and winter resting period. Plants must be mature and quite tall before they will bloom. 106♦

Notocactus ottonis
(Ball cactus)
- ● **Intermediate conditions**
- ● **For everyone**
- ● **Easy to bloom**

A small 4in (10cm) globe cactus, *N. ottonis* has large 1½in (4cm) yellow flowers in spring, several to a plant. Charming and worthwhile.

Grow at a sunny window; use a potting mix of equal parts of soil, sand and gravel. Topdress the surface of the soil mix with gravel to avoid any possibility of rot at the base of the plant. Keep evenly moist with soft water except in winter, when it needs a 4 to 8 week rest at cooler temperatures – about 60°F (16°C) – and less water. Do not feed. Repot only every fourth year. This plant likes good ventilation, and is sure to bloom if given winter rest and sun. Grow new plants from offsets or from seed; start both in spring.

To encourage bloom:
Grow in small pots and provide a definite winter rest. 106♦

Odontioda
- ● **Cool conditions**
- ● **For beginners**
- ● **Easy to bloom**

These hybrids of *Odontoglossum* and *Coohlioda*, up to 12in (30cm) tall, are robust plants with dark green leaves and colorful flowers, as many as 6 or 8 to a stem. There are many varieties, so colors vary greatly, but they are generally mauve-purple. Blooms are stunning and appear in summer and autumn. Flowers can be cut, and will stay fresh in a vase for a week or more.

Grow these orchids in a bright but never sunny place; the plants need good light but direct sun will harm them quickly. Use a potting mix of medium-grade fir bark kept moist all year. Do not feed. Spray plants with tepid water frequently during hot weather. These are cool-loving orchids and heat quickly desiccates them. They prefer temperatures of 50°F (10°C) at night. Get new plants by division in spring.

To encourage bloom:
Grow cool and well-ventilated. 107♦

Odontoglossum grande
(Clown orchid; tiger orchid)
- ● **Cool conditions**
- ● **For beginners**
- ● **Easy to bloom**

A popular 18in (45cm) orchid, *O. grande* has leathery dark green leaves, and bears lovely 6in (15cm) brown and yellow flowers in summer that last for several weeks. This is one of the finest orchids for home growing and requires little special care. Ideal for beginners.

Grow the tiger orchid in a bright window. Pot in clay containers, using medium-grade fir bark. Keep the bark moist with lime-free water all year except in winter, when moisture can be reduced somewhat. Provide adequate humidity but do not directly spray the plants, as the bulbs can rot with excessive moisture and gray days. Do not feed. Repot every fourth year.

After plants bloom, allow a definite resting time, keeping the bark barely moist. When new growth starts, increase watering. Rarely bothered by insects. Get new plants by division, or from orchid suppliers.

To encourage bloom:
Observe a 6–7 week rest. 109♦

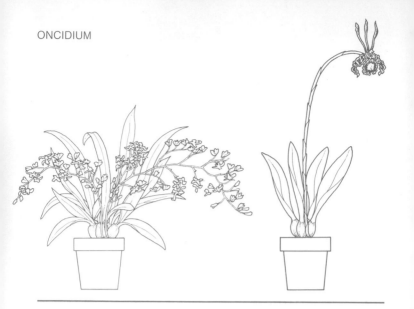

Oncidium ornithorhynchum
- Cool conditions
- For beginners
- Easy to bloom

Oncidium papilio
(Butterfly orchid)
- Intermediate conditions
- For everyone
- Easy to bloom

A charming small orchid about 24in (60cm) tall, with blue-green leaves, *O. ornithorhynchum* bears sprays of tiny lilac-pink fragrant flowers in autumn and winter, hundreds to a plant. Nice spot of color for the indoor garden. Very attractive and desirable and easy to grow.

Grow this orchid at a bright exposure – a west or east window is fine. Pot in medium-grade fir bark. Be sure drainage is good. Water freely in summer months, but not so much the rest of the year. Do not feed. Provide ample humidity (40 percent) and good ventilation. Let the plant rest after flowering. New plants from suppliers or division.

To encourage bloom:
Give winter rest of 4–8 weeks.

A fine 18in (45cm) orchid with thick succulent leaves, *O. papilio* bears one handsome 5in (12.5cm) chesnut brown-and-yellow flower per stalk in summer. Mature plants may have several flowers, opening one at a time in succession. A good accent plant at the window.

Grow the butterfly orchid at a bright window – sun is not necessary. Use a potting soil of medium fir bark; small pots are best. Keep the bark evenly moist all year. Do not feed. Provide adequate humidity (40 percent) and be sure the plant is in a well ventilated area. Flowers last a long time cut and placed in a vase of water. A care-free plant sure to please. New plants from orchid suppliers or by division.

To encourage bloom:
Provide good air circulation.

Pachystachys lutea
(Golden hops; golden shrimp plant; lollipop plant)
● **Intermediate conditions**
● **For everyone**
● **Easy to bloom**

Sometimes known as Jacobinia or Beloperone, this 20in (50cm) plant has lance shaped dark green leaves, and yellow bracts contrasting with white flowers in late summer. It is an easy plant to grow and fine indoors.

Grow at a bright window – an east or west exposure is fine. Use a potting mix of equal parts of soil and humus that drains readily. Water plant freely in warm weather, but allow to dry out between waterings the rest of the year. Feed monthly during warm weather. Prune back occasionally: cut off tip growth 4–6in (10–15cm) to encourage bushiness. After 2 years, start new plants from cuttings in spring. This plant has a tendency to legginess after a time.

To encourage bloom:
No special requirements. 108♦

Paphiopedilum maudiae
(Lady's slipper orchid; slipper orchid; Venus' slipper)
● **Cool conditions**
● **For everyone**
● **Easy to bloom**

This 16in (40cm) orchid is a hybrid between *P. callosum* and *P. lawrenceanum*. Leaves are light green and marbled; flowers appear in summer, and are white with delicate green shadings. A very pretty pot plant, and dependable to bloom every year – a real find for the indoor garden.

Grow this orchid at a west or east window – avoid direct sun on the plant. Use a potting mix of equal parts of medium-grade fir bark and soil that drains readily. Water evenly all year. Provide adequate humidity (30 percent) and mist the plant with water occasionally. Do not feed. It is rarely bothered by insects. Propagate by careful division once the flowers have died.

To encourage bloom:
Provide good ventilation and adequate humidity.

Parodia sanguiniflora
(Prairie fire cactus; Tom Thumb cactus)
- **Warm conditions**
- **For beginners**
- **Easy to bloom**

This pretty little cactus grows to 3in (7.5cm) across, pale green with a white wooly top and white spines. Brilliant red flowers in summer make this a spectacular plant.

Grow in a sunny window. Use a potting mix of equal parts of soil and humus – it likes a rich soil. Be sure drainage is good. Water sparingly, even during growth; too much water can cause rot. In winter, rest in a cool place (50°F, 10°C) and keep the soil just barely moist. Do not feed. Excellent for growing under artificial light. Grow new plants from offsets, seed or buy from suppliers.

To encourage bloom:
Give plenty of sun.

Passiflora caerulea
(Blue passion flower; common passion flower; passion vine)
- **Cool conditions**
- **For everyone**
- **Difficult to bloom**

Known for its spectacular 3in (7.5cm) flower of beautiful white, blue and purple, this vine grows very rapidly and can become very large. Flowers appear in late summer, followed by attractive orange-yellow fruits. Excellent for and best suited to greenhouse growing.

It needs a fairly bright but not sunny place at the window. Grow in a large tub of packaged soil that drains readily. Water heavily during growth but less in winter, when the plant rests. Feed every 2 weeks when in growth. Supply a suitable trellis support. Grow new plants from cuttings or seed in spring.

To encourage bloom:
Give plenty of water. Rest in winter at 50°F (10°C). If leaves are produced at the expense of flowers, stop feeding and allow the plant to become potbound. It is quite natural for some of the leaves to turn yellow and drop off the plant. 108♦

Pelargonium
(Geranium)
● **Cool conditions**
● **For beginners**
● **Easy to bloom**

These are popular indoor plants with three main types; zonals (*P. zonale*), regals (*P. grandiflorum*), and the trailing, or ivy-leaved, geraniums (*P. peltatum*). Most are medium-sized plants up to 24in (60cm) tall, and flowers come in many colors, but mainly from the red end of the spectrum. A large versatile group of plants that thrive in cool conditions.

Plants like a sunny place, grow in a rich, slightly alkaline potting mixture of equal parts of humus and soil with some sand added. Be sure the medium drains readily. Water freely, then allow to dry out between waterings. Geraniums bloom best when potbound, so grow in small pots. All types rest in winter; water sparingly then, and do not feed. Keep them at 50°F (10°C). Feed every other week when in active growth. Avoid overwatering and high humidity; do not mist leaves and provide good ventilation. Grow new plants from seed or cuttings taken in spring for winter bloom; in autumn for spring or summer bloom. Discard old plants, which will decline in flowering vigor.

The line drawings show the typical form of the three main types of pelargonium. Above left: *P. zonale*; above: *P. grandiflorum*; below: *P. peltatum*. All will make ideal and easy to grow houseplants.

To encourage bloom:
Provide the cool period in winter. Keep in full sun and do not overwater or overfeed. Grow potbound for sumptuous blooms. 110–111

Pentas lanceolata
(Egyptian star cluster; Egyptian star flower)
● **Intermediate conditions**
● **For beginners**
● **Easy to bloom**

An overlooked plant but one with great beauty. Its showy umbels of pink flowers appear on and off throughout the warm months. Hybrids are available with purple and white flowers. Kept to 24in (60cm) with careful pruning, these plants make excellent indoor subjects and add great color to a window. Flowers last a long time when cut and put in a vase of water. Even small plants bloom so these are indeed worthy additions to the indoor garden. An ideal plant for beginners

Grow in sun. Use a standard houseplant soil kept evenly moist all year. Feed every 2 weeks when the plants are in active growth. Old plants have a tendency to get leggy so start new ones from stem cuttings taken every spring.

To encourage bloom:
Grow in small clay pots; likes to be potbound. Provide at least 4 hours of sunshine each day. 112♦

Phalaenopsis hybrids
(Moth orchid)
● **Intermediate conditions**
● **For everyone**
● **Easy to bloom**

A popular and beautiful orchid with straplike broad dark green leaves growing to 14in (35cm) and long stems of flat handsome white, pink or yellow flowers, usually in summer or autumn. It is a favorite of orchid enthusiasts. Flowers last for weeks and a mature plant may bear as many as 100 flowers. Impressive and sure to please.

Grow the moth orchid at a bright window – a west exposure is fine. Sun will desiccate this plant. Pot in medium-grade fir bark and provide excellent humidity (50 percent). Good ventilation is necessary as well. Water evenly throughout the year with a slight drying out in winter. Do not feed. The plant is rarely bothered by insects. New plants from suppliers or by division.

To encourage bloom:
Do not overwater. Allow plant a period of rest in winter. 129♦

Pleione formosana 'Snow White'
- Cool conditions
- For everyone
- Easy to bloom

This is a small terrestrial 10in (25cm) orchid with ribbed green leaves; it has lovely flowers in spring or sometimes in autumn. Plants make exceptionally good house subjects and grow easily in 4in (10cm) pots. A real find for houseplant enthusiasts, and sure to bloom even when grown in shaded corners.

Grow in a shady location – avoid strong sun. Pot in equal parts of medium-grade fir bark and soil, and keep uniformly moist except in winter, when a resting period of about 6 weeks with little water is advisable. It will tolerate and need coolness (50°F, 10°C). Do not feed. It is rarely bothered by insects. Grow new plants from bulbils in spring.

To encourage bloom:
Observe resting time. 112♦

Primula malacoides
(Baby primrose; fairy primrose)
- Cool conditions
- For beginners
- Easy to bloom

With wavy edged circular leaves, this 14in (35cm) plant bears lovely pink, red, purple or white flowers in winter and spring, making it a valuable addition to the indoor garden. Generally an outdoor plant, it also does well in the home if kept really cool. Nice seasonal color.

Select a somewhat shady place for this. Grow in standard houseplant soil that drains well. Keep soil moist to the touch; a dry soil will harm the plants. Feed every 2 weeks during the growing season. Grow cool (50°F, 10°C) if possible; warm weather can harm these plants. Occasionally attacked by red spider, so use appropriate remedies. Get new plants by sowing seed in spring.

To encourage bloom:
Keep soil quite moist during growing period. Good ventilation helps; preferably grow in a cold frame until buds appear, then bring the plants into a cool room in the house. 129♦

Primula obconica
(Primula)
● **Cool conditions**
● **For beginners**
● **Easy to bloom**

This fine pot plant from China, growing to 12in (30cm) in height, has round hairy leaves and 2in (5cm) purple, red, white or pink flowers in winter and spring. It is a very pretty indoor subject for cool conditions.

Grow in a bright window, or an exposure with a little sun. Keep temperatures as cool as possible (50–60°F, 10–16°C). Provide a soil of equal parts of sand, soil and humus – be sure drainage is perfect. Plants require a great deal of water when growing, not so much the rest of the year. This particular species has leaves that can cause a rash with some people, so handle with gloves. New plants should be started from seed every spring.

To encourage bloom:
Do not allow to dry out. Keep in a very cool and airy place. Feed weekly when about to flower.

Primula vulgaris/ acaulis
(Primrose)
● **Cool conditions**
● **For everyone**
● **Easy to bloom**

Clusters of yellow flowers make this pretty 8in (20cm) plant a desirable one for the window. Blooms appear in spring. Hybrids are available with flowers of various colors including white, pink, red and blue. Primroses make nice accent plants.

Grow in a bright but not sunny window – a west exposure is fine. Pot in packaged houseplant soil. Keep evenly moist all year except in winter, when a drying out is necessary. Feed every 2 weeks during growth. Provide good ventilation. Easily grown in coolness (55°F, 13°C). Grow new plants from seed in spring; they do well when raised under artificial light.

To encourage bloom:
Keep cool with good ventilation. Grow outside in cool shade after flowering if you want flowers again the following spring.

Above: **Phalaenopsis hybrids**
Now available in yellow, pink, white or 'peppermint' stripes like this P. Hennessy, these are the beauties of the orchid group. 126♦

Right: **Primula malacoides**
Whorls of rose-purple flowers make this outdoor plant an indoor favorite. Handsome wavy edged leaves. 127♦

Above: **Punica granatum 'Nana'**
Scarlet red flowers always create a sensation when you grow this miniature pomegranate. 145♦

Left: **Rechsteineria cardinalis**
An overlooked gesneriad, this fine plant has brilliant red 2in (5cm) flowers for many weeks in summer. Ideal size for windowsills. 146♦

Right: **Rebutia krainziana**
Tiny and charming, this ball cactus bears very large red flowers in the summer. Ideal for beginners. 145♦

Above left: **Schlumbergera
x buckleyi**
*An excellent plant for superb autumn
color and so easy to propagate from
simple stem cuttings. A must.* 148♦

Left: **Schizocentron elegans**
*Blooming at intervals through winter
into early summer, this is an easy
and colorful pot plant.* 147♦

Above and right: **Saintpaulia**
*A huge group of favorite plants with
varieties in many colors. Also
available as miniatures.* 147♦

Above: **Smithiantha cinnabarina**
*Lush green leaves and handsome
bell shaped orange-red flowers
make this plant welcome* 149♦

Below: **Schlumbergera gaertneri**
*Lovely scarlet flowers make this
forest dwelling cactus a must for all
indoor gardeners.* 148♦

Above: **Sinningia**
Many fine hybrids are now available, *all with brilliantly colored flowers that* *are stunning in bloom.* 149♦

Above: **Stanhopea wardii**
An unusual orchid with large leaves and waxy flowers borne from the bottom of the plant. Heavily scented with a pleasing fragrance. 151♦

Left: **Solanum capsicastrum**
Prized mainly for its orange fruits rather than its small white flowers, this compact plant brings color to the windowsill in winter. 150♦

Right: **Spathiphyllum 'Mauna Loa'**
Striking flowers, compact growth and ability to endure neglect make this recommended. 150♦

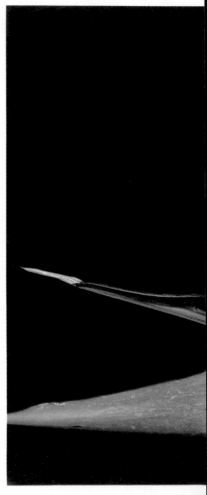

Right: **Streptocarpus hybrid**
If you want dazzling flowers look to the fine streptocarpus hybrids. Blooms come in wonderful shades of violet, pink or white. 153♦

Below: **Strelitzia reginae**
A stunning plant with 6in (15cm) blooms. Needs warmth and space. Spectacular but temperamental. 152♦

Above: **Thunbergia alata**
A colorful tropical vining plant that grows well in warm airy conditions. Difficult, but worthwhile. 153♦

Above: **Vallota speciosa**
A bulbous plant from South Africa, this beauty is easy to grow and quite spectacular in bloom. 155♦

Left: **Tulipa (Triumph type)**
These fine flowers can be forced during the winter to provide welcome color in the home. 155♦

Above right: **Trichopilia tortilis**
A fine indoor orchid that really does grow and bloom indoors. Unusual flowers with corkscrew petals. 154♦

Right: **Stephanotis floribunda**
It is hard to beat the fragrance of Madagascar jasmine. White star shaped 1in (2.5cm) flowers appear in clusters in summer. 152♦

141

Above: **Vriesea splendens**
This favorite bromeliad offers not only striking foliage but also a long-lasting 'sword' of red bracts. 157♦

Below: **Vanda suavis** var. **tricolor**
This beautiful orchid from Java and Bali produces fragrant waxy flowers during summer and autumn. 156♦

Above: **Zephyranthes candida**
*Zephyr lilies are pretty and bear
graceful flowers during the summer*
*and into the autumn. Flower color is
usually white, but orange and pink
varieties are also seen.* 158♦

Above: **Zygopetalum crinitum**
Another popular orchid, this one bears lovely fragrant green and *purple flowers in midwinter. A welcome addition to any indoor garden. Ideal for beginners.* 158▸

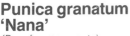

Punica granatum 'Nana'
(Dwarf pomegranate)
- **Intermediate conditions**
- **For beginners**
- **Easy to bloom**

A fine miniature indoor tree, growing to about 14in (35cm) in a pot, the dwarf pomegranate has tiny green leaves, and large bell shaped scarlet flowers in summer followed by small yellow inedible fruits. It is a charming plant for indoors and does well with little care. Plants make handsome bonsai subjects and can be trained with little problem. In summer the pomegranate appreciates an outdoor vacation on a sunny patio or terrace, where it can add beauty to the scene. If this is not possible, ensure that plants kept indoors have good ventilation.

Grow the dwarf pomegranate at a bright and sunny window. Use equal parts of soil and humus for a potting medium. Keep evenly moist throughout the summer and feed every 2 weeks. Rarely bothered by insects. Propagate by heeled stem cuttings or seed in spring.

To encourage bloom:
Keep cool in winter (45°F, 7°C) and reduce amount of water. 130♦

Rebutia krainziana
(Crown cactus)
- **Warm conditions**
- **For beginners**
- **Easy to bloom**

This miniature cactus is a gem, growing to 2in (5cm) in diameter, with bright red flowers in a circular pattern in summer. It is one of the dependable cacti, sure to please, and it grows under adverse conditions. There are many fine species of *Rebutia*, most of which have red flowers.

This plant needs ample sun in summer to bear flowers, so grow it at a sunny window. Use equal parts of sand and soil for potting and allow 1in (2.5cm) at the top of the pot for a layer of gravel. Water copiously in spring and summer but the rest of the year keep somewhat dry. Feed once a month in warm weather, but not at all the rest of the year. Plants seem immune to any insect attack. Propagate by seeds or offsets.

To encourage bloom:
Give plenty of sun. 131♦

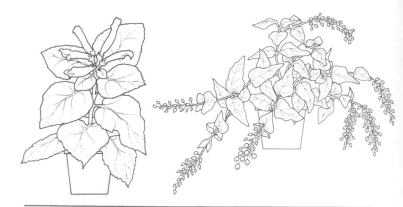

Rechsteineria cardinalis
(Cardinal flower)
● **Intermediate conditions**
● **For everyone**
● **Easy to bloom**

An overlooked gesneriad, growing to 24in (60cm), with handsome dark green heart shaped leaves, and brilliant red flowers in summer. The tubular flowers are unusual and highly decorative. An easy indoor plant, sure to please. This is a good plant for the windowsill, neither too large nor too small.

Grow at a bright window, as they like light, but sun can be harmful; a west window is usually ideal. Pot in a loose mix of equal parts of soil and humus, and water heavily in warm weather, not so much the rest of the year. Feed every 2 weeks during growth; provide 50 percent humidity. After plants bloom, leave the tubers in the pot and store them dry in a shady place at 55°F (13°C). Let them rest for about 4 months. When new growth starts, repot for next season. Use small pots. Start new plants from seed or division of tubers in spring.

To encourage bloom:
Keep in a cool place in winter. 130●

Rivina humilis
(Baby pepper; bloodberry; rouge plant)
● **Intermediate conditions**
● **For everyone**
● **Easy to bloom**

A fine bushy plant growing to 24in (60cm), with thin textured leaves, and erect spikes of tiny pinkish white flowers blooming from summer to autumn. Red berries follow the flowers to give an extra bonus of color for the indoor garden.

Grow in a bright location – a west window is fine. Pot in packaged soil that drains readily. Water freely in summer, but less during the rest of the year. Feed every 2 weeks when in growth. Provide good ventilation. It is sometimes attacked by red spider; use an appropriate remedy. Grow new plants from seed or cuttings started in spring – artificial light is fine during this early period.

To encourage bloom:
No special requirements.

Saintpaulia
(African violet)
● **Intermediate conditions**
● **For everyone**
● **Easy to bloom**

These immensely popular gesneriads are free-flowering and dependable indoor plants

Grow African violets at a bright but not sunny window in an area of good air circulation. A little winter sun is fine. Use standard houseplant soil that drains readily, and small pots. Water the soil moderately to keep it slightly moist but never wet. Use tepid water; allow it to stand overnight in a watering can. Feed once a month in spring, summer and autumn; plant food rich in superphosphate will be particularly beneficial. Do not get water on the foliage, it will leave ugly marks. Dry air causes leaf curl and bud drop so maintain good humidity (but do not spray the plants). Turn the plants a quarter round monthly so that all the leaves get light. Easily propagated from leaf cuttings in spring.

To encourage bloom:
Do not pamper – allow to grow naturally. If few flowers are produced, pick them off and keep the plant on a dry regime for 6 weeks. This should induce bloom. 133♦

Schizocentron elegans
(Spanish shawl)
● **Intermediate conditions**
● **For beginners**
● **Easy to bloom**

This is a thoroughly delightful 12in (30cm) plant with dark green hairy leaves and pretty pink-purple flowers, 1in (2.5cm) across, starting in late winter and continuing colorful until early summer. Makes a fine hanging basket plant.

Grow the Spanish shawl in a bright location – a west window is fine. Use a standard houseplant soil and clay pots are best so that water evaporates slowly from the soil. Keep soil reasonably moist all year, never too dry nor too wet. Feed every 2 weeks in warm weather, once a month at other times. Occasionally, trim back the plant to encourage new growth – cut off 3 to 4in (7.5–10cm) of tip growth. Rarely bothered by insects. All in all a very amenable indoor plant. New plants from division of rooted shoots.

To encourage bloom:
Grow potbound. 132♦

Schlumbergera × buckleyi
(Zygocactus truncatus)
(Crab cactus; lobster cactus)
● **Intermediate conditions**
● **For beginners**
● **Easy to bloom**

The crab cactus grows to about 30in (75cm), and has toothed branches that distinguish it from *Schlumbergera gaertneri.*Dozens of flowers appear in autumn, and a mature plant is a fine sight. Excellent for hanging baskets. Many varieties are available, in different colors – red, pink, orange, white.

Grow this jungle type cactus at a bright but not sunny window; it does not like direct sun. Use a potting mix of equal parts of medium-grade fir bark and soil. Keep plants moderately moist except in autumn, when roots should be fairly dry and plants grown quite cool (55 °F, 13 °C) with 12 hours of uninterrupted darkness each day for a month to encourage flower buds. Do not feed. Pieces of stem root easily in sand for new plants. Allow cuttings to dry first.

To encourage bloom:
Observe period of darkness. Do not move plants about – it causes the buds to fall. 132◗

Schlumbergera gaertneri
(Rhipsalidopsis gaertneri)
(Leaf cactus; link-leaf cactus)
● **Intermediate conditions**
● **For beginners**
● **Easy to bloom**

The leaf cactus is a fine epiphytic plant growing to 24in (60cm) and has scalloped branches that distinguish it from toothed *Zygocactus* varieties. Red flowers in spring.

Grow this cactus at a sunny window in autumn and winter – in bright light the rest of the year. For a potting mix use equal parts of lime-free soil and medium-grade fir bark for the best results. In spring and summer water plants freely with lime-free water, but in autumn and winter reduce watering. Feed monthly. In the autumn or early winter give plants 12 hours of uninterrupted darkness per day, and cool nights (55 °F, 13 °C), and they will set buds. When buds form, return the plant to the window. Provide good humidity (40 percent); spray with water in warm months. Propagate by cuttings in spring.

To encourage bloom:
Must have a period of darkness with cool, dry conditions. Do not move plants or the buds will drop. 134◗

Sinningia
(Gloxinia)
- **Cool conditions**
- **For a challenge**
- **Difficult to bloom**

Smithiantha cinnabarina
(Temple bells)
- **Warm conditions**
- **For everyone**
- **Easy to bloom**

These glamorous Brazilian plants up to 12in (30cm) tall have single or double tubular flowers in vivid colors.

Gloxinias like a location where there is subdued light, and sun is not necessary to promote flowering. Grow plants in equal parts of soil and humus. Start the tubers in spring or autumn, using one to a 5in (12.5cm) clay pot. Set the tuber hollow side up and cover with soil (but only just). Keep evenly moist at a temperature of about 60 °F (16 °C). When growth starts, increase the watering somewhat and move the plant to a slightly warmer location.

When the flowers fade, gradually decrease watering, remove tops, and store tubers in a dry place at 55 °F (13 °C). Keep soil barely moist and rest from 6 to 8 weeks (no more) or tubers lose their vitality. Repot in fresh soil. Propagate from basal shoot cuttings, leaf cuttings or seed.

To encourage bloom:
Observe resting time. Feed weekly when flower buds form. 135▶

A fine 24in (60cm) gesneriad with large lush green leaves, and handsome bell shaped flowers from autumn through winter, when color is so needed at windows. The orange-red flowers are exquisite. Plants adjust well to indoor conditions. Dependable. Many hybrids in vivid colors.

Grow temple bells at a bright window, but no sun is necessary. Be sure the air circulation is good. Use a potting mix of equal parts of soil and humus that drains readily. In early spring start each rhizome in a 4–5in (10–12.5cm) pot, planting 1in (2.5cm) deep. Keep the soil evenly moist. After the flowers fade, store the rhizome dry in the pot in a cool shaded place at 55 °F (13 °C) for about 3 months. Then repot and return to the bright window. Propagate from seed, division of rhizomes or from leaf cuttings.

To encourage bloom:
Observe resting time. Feed weekly when flower buds appear. 134▶

Solanum capsicastrum
(Jerusalem cherry; winter cherry)
- **Intermediate conditions**
- **For beginners**
- **Easy to bloom**

A small dark-leaved shrub from Brazil, the Jerusalem cherry grows up to 15in (38cm) tall and has white starry flowers in summer followed by non-edible fruits that stay on the plant well into winter. They ripen through green and yellow to red.

Grow the Jerusalem cherry in a bright window – a west or east exposure is fine. Use standard houseplant soil that drains readily. Keep the soil evenly moist except in winter, when plants can be grown somewhat dry and cool (55 °F, 13 °C), without letting them dry out completely. Plants like an airy place. Mist leaves daily with water. Rarely bothered by insects. Generally good for the season only and then must be discarded or placed in the garden and pruned back to 8in (20cm); it can then be brought inside before the first frost. New plants from seed.

To encourage bloom:
Pollinate the flowers by hand using a brush. Keep plants cool during fruiting. Replace plants after 2 years. The fruits are poisonous. 136♦

Spathiphyllum 'Mauna Loa'
(Peace lily; spathe flower; white flag; white sails)
- **Intermediate conditions**
- **For everyone**
- **Easy to bloom**

This plant from South America has shiny green leaves and white spathe flowers that resemble anthuriums. Plants grow up to 18in (45cm) tall. In good growing conditions this hybrid will produce fragrant flowers intermittently throughout the year. Although spathiphyllums are not spectacular plants, they seem to adjust to almost any indoor location and do well.

Grow these at any exposure – they can tolerate sun or shade. Use standard houseplant soil. Allow the soil to dry out between waterings. Use a plant food about 4 times a year. Plants are rarely bothered by insects and seem trouble free. For a good show grow in 12in (30cm) pots. Excellent room plants even in shady corners. Propagate by seed or division of the rhizomes in spring.

To encourage bloom:
Keep warm and humid. 137♦

Sprekelia formosissima
(Aztec lily; Jacobean lily)
- Cool conditions
- For beginners
- Easy to bloom

This bulbous plant has narrow strap shaped leaves usually appearing after the flowers. The flowers are bright scarlet, exotic in appearance, and borne on 18–24in (45–60cm) stems in late spring or early summer. A very dependable plant and a real beauty for the indoor garden.

Grow this lily in sun. Pot the bulbs, two thirds buried, in equal parts of soil and humus that drains readily. Water freely while in growth. Do not feed. When leaves yellow, let the soil go almost dry and rest for several weeks. Repot in fresh soil in autumn. Grow new plants from the small bulbs that form next to the main one. Remove these in the autumn.

To encourage bloom:
No special requirements.

Stanhopea wardii
- Warm conditions
- For beginners
- Easy to bloom

This unusual orchid from Mexico, Central and South America grows to 24in (60cm) in height; it has large dark green leaves, and bears pendent flower spikes in late summer. Flowers are up to 5in (12.5cm) across, white or yellow with brown markings, and heavily scented. The plant blooms from the bottom of the pot so open orchid baskets or clay pots with several large drainage holes are necessary.

Grow at a bright but not sunny window – good light is needed to encourage flowers. Pot in medium-grade fir bark – basket culture is recommended and drainage must be perfect. Flood with water in the warm months but in winter allow plants to be fairly dry. Do not feed. Provide adequate humidity (40 percent) and good ventilation. Rarely bothered by insects. Buy new plants from suppliers or divide the pseudobulbs during the summer.

To encourage bloom:
Give plenty of water in growth. 136♦

151

Stephanotis floribunda
(Madagascar jasmine)
- Intermediate conditions
- For a challenge
- Difficult to bloom

Here is a fine plant for the indoor garden, with handsome dark green leaves, and scented white flowers in midsummer. Plants climb, so supply a suitable support. Very pretty. One plant can perfume an entire room. Somewhat difficult to grow but not impossible and worth a try. Plants will grow to 10ft (3m).

Plants thrive in an east or west window – they must have bright light but sun is not necessary. Pot in equal parts of soil and humus. Keep soil evenly moist with lime-free water all year except in winter, when it can be slightly drier. Provide adequate moisture by misting with water. Feed every 2 weeks in summer. Watch for mealy bugs, which sometimes attack plants (use appropriate remedies). Propagate by cuttings in spring.

To encourage bloom:
Must have coolness (55°F, 13°C) in winter resting period. Do not move the plant or the buds will drop. 141♦

Strelitzia reginae
(Bird of paradise flower)
- Warm conditions
- For a challenge
- Difficult to bloom

Called 'bird of paradise' because its flowers resemble exotic birds, this 40in (1m) plant has gray-green spatulate leaves, and bright orange and purple flowers in summer. Only mature plants with 7 or more leaves bloom and then reluctantly indoors. Even so, it is worth a try because of the spectacular flowers.

Grow this plant at your sunniest window – it must have at least 3 hours of sun daily to prosper. Use a standard houseplant soil and feed every 2 weeks in summer, but not at all the rest of the year. In winter keep cool at 50°F (10°C) and allow the soil to dry out somewhat, but in summer flood the plants with water. Use large tubs. Rarely bothered by insects. Propagate by division of tubers or from seed; either way new plants will take several years to flower.

To encourage bloom:
Buy mature plants. Leave undisturbed – dividing plants stops flowering for several years. 139♦

Streptocarpus hybrids

(Cape primrose; Cape cowslip)
- **Intermediate conditions**
- **For everyone**
- **Easy to bloom**

There is a fine new group of hybrids available that bloom almost all year, but mainly in the summer. Flower colors are white, pink or violet, and the tubular flowers are indeed handsome. Plants grow to about 8–12in (20–30cm) in height. Highly recommended.

Grow the Cape primrose in a bright window, protected from direct sun. Use standard houseplant soil that drains readily; feed every 2 weeks when in growth. After a bloom cycle reduce watering, let the plant rest for about 4–6 weeks, and then resume watering. Always use lime-free water. Do not mist the leaves; water on the foliage can cause rot. Repot annually for best results. Grow new plants from seed or leaf cuttings taken in midsummer.

To encourage bloom:
Allow to rest slightly after blooming. Replace plants after 2 or 3 years as they decline in flowering vigor. 139♦

Thunbergia alata

(Black-eyed Susan vine; clock vine)
- **Warm conditions**
- **For a challenge**
- **Difficult to bloom**

This uncommonly beautiful plant, with funnel shaped yellow-orange flowers and attractive green foliage, climbs up to 10ft (3m). It makes a happy note of color in midsummer at the window, but is a difficult plant to keep from year to year. In some climates it may be easier to treat it as an annual and raise new plants from seed each year. Good for spot color only. Excellent hanging basket plant.

Grow this at your sunniest window – it will not bear flowers in shade. Use a standard houseplant soil that drains readily. Plants are greedy and need copious watering and feeding every 2 weeks during the warm months. Provide a suitable support and check the plant occasionally for insects – red spider mites are fond of the foliage. Use appropriate remedies. Maintain good humidity. Grow new plants from seed.

To encourage bloom:
Must have at least 3 hours of sun daily to bloom successfully. 138♦

153

Tillandsia cyanea
(Pink quill)
- **Intermediate conditions**
- **For a challenge**
- **Difficult to bloom**

This fine 10in (25cm) bromeliad has grassy dark green foliage and lovely purple flowers – dozens to a bract in early summer. Flowers last only a few days but are followed by others. A truly fine indoor plant.

Grow the pink quill in a bright location – a west window is excellent. Use equal parts of lime-free soil and small-grade fir bark for potting. Keep the medium evenly moist; do not feed. Plants need excellent ventilation – they will not thrive in a stagnant atmosphere. Provide ample humidity; spray leaves with tepid water during warm weather. Rarely bothered by insects. Get new plants from suppliers or from rooted offsets detached from the parent plant.

To encourage bloom:
Keep humid.

Trichopilia tortilis
(Corkscrew orchid)
- **Intermediate conditions**
- **For everyone**
- **Easy to bloom**

Don't let the name fool you – this is an exquisite 14in (35cm) orchid that does better in the home than in a greenhouse. Plants have narrow dark green leaves and 5in (12.5cm) tubular white flowers spotted in orange with corkscrew petals – very handsome. Blooms last several weeks in spring or autumn, and are undemanding. A very fine plant that should be in every indoor garden.

Grow this orchid in a bright place. Use small-grade fir bark and pot somewhat tightly. Keep the bark evenly moist at all times of the year. Mist with water to provide adequate humidity and be sure the plant is in a place where there is good air circulation. Do not feed. Repot only every third year – this plant does not like to be disturbed. Rarely bothered by insects. Get new plants from suppliers or divide pseudobulbs.

To encourage bloom:
Do not overwater. 141▸

Tulipa
(Tulip)
- **Cool conditions**
- **For everyone**
- **Easy to bloom**

These plants need little introduction, and their handsome flowers are available in dozens of colors. The best tulips for indoor cultivation are the early dwarf varieties, which grow to about 12in (30cm) tall; choose single or double flowered varieties.

Grow tulips in your sunniest place. Use a potting mix of equal parts of sand and soil that drains readily. Pot bulbs in autumn (covering completely) and keep cool (50 °F, 10 °C) and shaded until the flower buds begin to show color; then move them into warmer, bright conditions. High temperatures while plants are in bud will cause the buds to die off. Water sparingly, keeping mix just moist. Start new bulbs each year.

To encourage bloom:
Grow in cool conditions. 140♦

Vallota speciosa
(Scarborough lily)
- **Cool conditions**
- **For everyone**
- **Easy to bloom**

A bulbous plant with strap leaves, *V. speciosa* has bright scarlet funnel shaped flowers 3in (7.5cm) across on 24in (60cm) stems in summer. A spectacular plant.

Grow in sun. Pot in equal parts of soil and humus that drains readily. Use a 4 or 5in (10–12.5cm) clay pot and leave the top of the bulb uncovered. Water evenly throughout the year, never too much or too little. Do not feed. Maintain good ventilation and humidity of 30 percent. Plants can be grown in the same container for several years. Grow new plants from seeds or from the offset bulbs that develop beside the parent bulb. Remove in autumn.

To encourage bloom:
Do not overwater. 140♦

Vanda suavis var. tricolor

- **Intermediate conditions**
- **For everyone**
- **Easy to bloom**

This popular vanda grows to 48in (120cm) or more with long straplike leaves: flowers are 4in (10cm) across, usually white and spotted with red and purple. As many as 10 flowers to a scape are borne on mature plants in summer or autumn. Excellent plant if you have the space.

Like most vandas, this one needs sunshine at its best so place it at a sunny exposure. Use a potting mix of large-grade fir bark kept moist most of the year. Do not feed. A slight drying out is permissible in winter. Maintain excellent ventilation and mist plant with tepid water occasionally to maintain humidity. This plant is relatively free of insects. Propagate from side shoots.

To encourage bloom:
Must have sun. 142◊

Veltheimia viridifolia
(Forest lily)

- **Cool conditions**
- **For everyone**
- **Easy to bloom**

This 20in (50cm) bulbous plant from the lily family is hard to beat for winter color. It has large dark green glossy leaves and a yellow-green to rosy pink cone of small flowers borne at the tip of a tall stem. Not to be missed and a dependable houseplant.

Grow in bright light – almost any exposure is fine. Pot in standard houseplant soil in 8in (20cm) pots. Place one bulb to a pot with the top 1/4in (6mm) extended above the soil line. Be sure drainage is good. Keep soil moist except after flowering, when the plant can be kept somewhat dry and moved to a cooler location, 50 °F (10 °C). Feed monthly when in growth. Increase watering as growth starts, and after flowering allow to die back and rest through the summer months. Repot in fresh soil in early autumn for new flowers. Grow new plants from offset bulbs that develop next to the main bulb.

To encourage bloom:
Observe summer rest period.

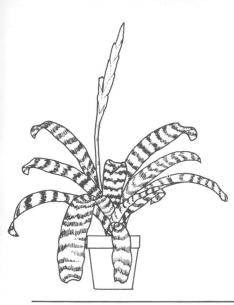

Vriesea splendens
(Flaming sword)
- **Intermediate conditions**
- **For everyone**
- **Easy to bloom**

A rosette shaped bromeliad, *V. splendens* has glossy green leaves banded with brown, and a sword shaped spike up to 18in (45cm) tall, bearing bright red bracts and yellow flowers, that appears in summer and lasts for weeks. The plant is more unusual in appearance than pretty, but its vibrant color makes it a popular indoor subject. Easy to grow.

Grow the flaming sword at a sunny window – it likes light. Use a potting mix of equal parts of medium-grade fir bark and soil. Keep the center of the plant filled with water, and the soil moist to the touch. Provide an airy place. Mist the leaves to furnish adequate humidity. Never bothered by insects. Grow new plants from offsets at the base of the parent plant: remove these when they are 3in (7.5cm) tall and have developed roots, and pot in separate containers.

To encourage bloom:
No special requirements. 142♦

Zantedeschia rehmannii
(Calla lily; pink arum; pink calla; trumpet lily)
- **Cool conditions**
- **For beginners**
- **Easy to bloom**

This tuberous plant growing to 20in (50cm) in height has handsome spear shaped leaves, and pink to cream flower spathes in summer. Generally grown outdoors, it also makes a fine pot plant indoors.

Grow this calla lily in bright light until foliage develops, and then move it to a sunny window for bloom. Use a potting mix of equal parts of soil and humus that drains readily. Water moderately at first, and when growth appears keep the soil fairly moist. Plant one tuber to a 4–5in (10–12.5cm) pot. Give liquid plant food once a month. After flowering, allow tubers to ripen off naturally by reducing water. Then rest in pots in a cool shady place at 50 °F (10 °C) and withhold water entirely. In spring repot the bulbs in fresh soil. Grow new plants from tiny offshoots or by dividing the tubers when repotting.

To encourage bloom:
Observe the strict resting time. Do not omit feeding.

157

Zephyranthes candida
(Fairy lily; flowers of the western wind; rain lily; swamp lily; zephyr lily; zephyr flower)
- **Cool conditions**
- **For a challenge**
- **Difficult to bloom**

Growing only to 12in (30cm), the zephyr lily has grassy foliage, and pretty white flowers in summer. There are also pink and orange varieties. These overlooked plants do very well indoors.

The zephyr lily needs a sunny window; in spring pot 4 or 5 bulbs to a 6in (15cm) pot. Cover completely with a mix of equal parts of soil and humus that drains readily. Let the soil dry out between waterings. Do not feed. In winter, store the bulbs dry in a cool shaded place. Repot in fresh soil in spring. Bulbs are good for about three seasons. Grow new plants from offset bulbs that develop beside the main bulb.

To encourage bloom:
Observe resting time. 143♦

Zygopetalum crinitum
- **Intermediate conditions**
- **For beginners**
- **Easy to bloom**

A handsome orchid growing to 20in (50cm), this plant has papery green leaves, and exquisite flowers of green, purple and brown in winter. Flowers last several weeks on the plant. This is an overlooked but beautiful orchid.

Grow at a bright window; sun will harm this plant. Pot in medium-grade fir bark kept reasonably moist but never wet, and provide good ventilation. Keep humidity at about 40 percent. Do not feed. When growth stops in autumn (when the leaves are fully expanded), rest the plant without water and only an occasional misting. Sometimes the leaves develop black streaks and are unsightly, but the plants are not unhealthy. Get new plants from suppliers or divide pseudobulbs.

To encourage bloom:
Do not overwater. Do not disturb plants – they resent repotting. 144♦

Index to Common Names

Picture Credits

The publishers wish to thank the following photographers and agencies who have supplied photographs for this book. Photographs have been credited by page number and position on the page:
(B) Bottom, (T) Top, (C) Center,
(BL) Bottom left, etc.

A–Z Botanical Collection: 10(T), 13(B),
34(BL), 138(L), 138–9(B), 141(B)
Pat Brindley: 42(BL), 44(BL), 79(B),
110(B), 111
Peter Chapman: 46, 70(BL), 100(T),
100–101(B), 106
Eric Crichton: Back endpaper, 8, 9, 12,
13(T), 14, 15, 16(T), 33, 34(T), 36, 37(T),
38, 42(T), 43, 44(T), 47, 48(BL), 65,
66(TL), 66–7(B), 68(TL), 72(B), 74(B),
75(B), 76(BL), 77, 79(TL), 80, 97, 98(B),
101(T), 102, 103(B), 104(T), 105(T), 107,
109, 112, 129(T), 134(T), 136, 137,
140(T), 141, 142(B), 144
Derek Fell: 139(T)
Kees Hageman: 68(BL)
B. J. van der Lans: 11(B), 78, 143
Gordon Rowley: 11
Daan Smit: Front endpaper, Title page, 39,
105(BR), 134(B), 140(BL)
Harry Smith Photograph Collection: Half
title page, 10(B), 72(T), 75(T), 79(TR),
98(T), 108(BL), 129(BR), 142(T)
Michael Warren: 41(B), 99, 103(T)

PRINTED IN BELGIUM BY
proost
INTERNATIONAL BOOK PRODUCTION

Miltonia 'Peach Blossom'